ROMANCING
THE SOUL

SECOND EDITION

ROMANCING THE SOUL

YOUR PERSONAL GUIDE TO LIVING FREE

BOB TRASK

MEDIA

Published 2022 by Gildan Media LLC
aka G&D Media
www.GandDmedia.com

Front cover design by Tom McKeveny

Interior design by Meghan Day Healey of Story Horse, LLC

Library of Congress Cataloging-in-Publication Data is available upon request

ISBN: 978-1-7225-0509-7

10   9   8   7   6   5   4   3   2   1

CONTENTS

◇◇◇◇◇◇

INTRODUCTION

◇◇◇◇◇◇

Some years ago, as I was researching the most practical paths to higher consciousness for my students, I became aware that, for the past 200,000 years we have had only three ways of experiencing life—*Being, Doing,* and *Having.* I closed my eyes, leaned back, and contemplated the simplicity of those states, looking at them from every angle and thinking of how they connected. Then something shifted—they began flowing together and merged into an amazing and dynamic pattern that painted itself in my mind as a Triangle. Humbled and thrilled, I opened my eyes and began writing. As the pattern unfolded before me I saw how it would enrich and uplift lives. It was the ultimate map to success; simple to learn and easy to apply. It would also instill ever-expanding levels of clarity, courage, and confidence.

Professional athletes, performing artists, business leaders, and students in numerous countries all champion the Triangle because it has transformed their lives. Many of them have become my heroes and in this book are some of their stories. As you read these pages you will, as they did, recall the sacred desires you shelved because of impossible obstacles. Now, rather than impossible obstacles, every challenge you encounter will take you closer to your goals. With these proven techniques, today you may actually create the life of your dreams.

FOREWORD

Who are we, what are we doing here, where are we going, and how can we fulfill our lives? As a seeker and a scientist I have searched for answers to these questions most of my life; through university degrees in psychology and neuroscience, through extensive laboratory research on the relationships between brain and behavior, through studies in comparative religions, and through extensive participation in personal-growth programs.

Here, at last, is the jewel I have been searching for: *Romancing the Soul*, this precise, nonreligious integration of psychology and spirituality has answered my questions and become my handbook for living free. This amazing mind-spirit synthesis is so clearly written, so simply described, it becomes the foundation for Trask's Triangle; the core of his book and his work. Developed over thirty years, through the lives of thousands of people, Trask's Triangle is now a daily guide for families, businesses, performers, leaders and athletes around the world who want to live their dreams. Bob Trask believes that we must fulfill those dreams in order to complete our life's divine missions. Through an expansion of clarity and peace of mind, this process changes self-sabotaging tendencies and allows our souls to lead us. This training manual for spiritually harnessing the power of the Universe explains, step by step, the techniques that have created lives of personal freedom and success for people around the world. Here now, is his gift to us, presented in his enjoyable and thought-provoking style. Follow this simple guide and you will feel your life being renewed every day.

—Richard T. Robertson, Ph.D.
Professor and Chair,
Department of Anatomy and Neurobiology
University of California, Irvine, CA

THE INSPIRATION:
A WISE WOMAN SPEAKS

◇◇◇◇◇◇◇

We sat on the forest floor watching her and listening. A brook giggled over polished stones while tall trees leaning against the afternoon sky watched over us like guardians. From far away came the first deep rolling of thunder. Tia Maria leaned forward, tucking a strand of white hair behind an ear and watched the water weave around her feet.

"You know why you become so confused? You think you are a physical being with a soul. The opposite is the truth, of course; you are a soul with a physical being. As pure soul, you want to experience and express yourself, so you create a mind, and your mind needs a physical body, so it creates one. So now here you are in this wonderful world free to experience and express as you like. There is no blueprint for you to follow; you can create it as you go.

"And if you become afraid you might get greedy or selfish and hurt others. Those mistakes are painful, and embarrassing, but they are important because they remind us who we are and they get us back on our paths. Do you need to be forgiven for them? Children, you are automatically forgiven as you forgive others."

She looked up at the thunderclouds towering above us. "Look, pretty soon, a bolt of lightning is going to tear across that sky. What will we see up there then? A wound? A scar? No, the sky will heal instantly. And fish will shatter the perfect surface of a pond, but will the pond be damaged? No, it will heal. You are a perfect part of this Universe; when you are following your life's mission, you are flowing with that same grace as the sky and the pond and will be instantly healed and forgiven. But if you forget who you are, if you abandon your mission, you will fall from grace. Then your life will become unbalanced and you will suffer, but your pain is not punishment—it is Great Spirit waking you up, pushing you back onto your mission; back into your joy."

The old saint sat in her silence. We waited and the thunder came closer; soon the storm would be upon us. Without hurrying, Tia Maria dipped her hand in the brook, brought its cool water up to pat on her face and her eyes filled with tenderness. She spoke slowly to make sure we understood. "You are each a part of Great Spirit, of God, here on your personal mission. You worship by being true to yourself, by following your soul's calling. Don't be so concerned about loving God, let God love you. Your soul knows the way, let it lead and you will be filled with grace and your life will be a gift to the world."

CHAPTER ONE

LOST SOULS

◇◇◇◇◇◇

A life well-lived is a life filled with failure. But failure is not fatal, it is a blessing. The more precious our goal, the more failures and self-expansions we must undergo to attain it. We are on divine missions, each of us, without blueprints to follow; we are pioneers, designing our path as we go, reaching into the darkness of the unknown to accomplish what our souls call us to do. If, in the process, we compare the number of our failures to the number of our wins, our self-confidence might crumble, because we will fail far more often than we will succeed. But if we see each failure as an important part of success, a necessary step to winning, and then we will not let failure define us. Then our fear of failure cannot keep us from taking the risks we must take in order to win.

Leon's Story

Moments before he died, Leon Ames, staring at the ceiling of my ambulance, answered my question. "Yeah, my boat! If I hadn't been so damn scared of what someone might say, I'd have built my boat." He turned to me, his face working, his voice tight, "God, how I wish I'd just gone ahead and built that boat."

For several months before this, I'd been asking people who were fully aware that they were dying and who had surrendered to their deaths, the same question; "When you look back now, do you have any regrets?" I wanted to know because I wondered if there might be something to be learned by those of us who still had time to take a different path.

I had heard a few others say basically the same thing, but it was Leon's reply that really got my attention; he was the third person in a space of two weeks who basically told me, "If I could do my life over, I would do what I wanted instead of listening to my fear."

After Leon was dead, I sat alone in the dark ambulance watching rain, like tears, crawling down the windshield. I knew Leon. Six months earlier, I had gone to his home to take his wife to the hospital. She died within days and, with her death, Leon's reason for living. When his sudden heart attack came I went to his home and found him strangely calm but deeply sad. Leon did not fear death, but its nearness opened an old wound he had kept hidden from himself for years. The agony he suffered for his loss, the realization that he had come into this life with something important to do which now he would never accomplish. It was too late. Leon Ames understood finally that he had not accomplished his life's mission. Was it just a boat? Was all his sorrow over having not built a boat? I wondered how a boat could be so important, So, he described it to me; and, it was then that I realized he had envisioned a genius hull design that perhaps no one had ever seen before. It was a hull that would move through the water as water itself, partnering with water instead of fighting it. Leon had a mind full of ideas and even as he lay dying, a light came into his eyes. His boat would move through the water with a grace and ease that would cause boat builders to transform their ideas of hulls and sails. The design came only through Leon's soul. As we are each unique, so are our creations! Leon's design could never be replicated by anyone else. Because of his fears, he had deprived us of ever having that design in our world; and he now knew it.

As I sat in the ambulance waiting for my partner to finish his paper work, questions crowded into my mind. Why do so many of us come to the end of our lives not knowing how to live; not even remembering our missions or what made us unique in the world? Is it because we feel obligated and are in resistance to the pressures of obligation? Is it because we really don't understand? Leon would insist now that our motivation should not be an obligation but an opportunity. He learned too late that he was given a gift that he never unwrapped. His life's mission, his passion, would have been to design and build his boat; there is nothing he would rather have been doing. Leon turned away from his mission because he believed he *should* be doing something else. But can our life's mission be as easy as that? Should we go about the world just doing what we want to do, what we are passionate about, and dismissing our obligations?

I could not help looking at my own life that afternoon; I had been drowning in a life I didn't want to lead; avoiding doing what I really wanted because I was afraid of failing my obligations to others. I wondered—would my last moments be like those of Leon and other dying people I had talked to? Would I be devastated to find that the fair had left town, while I still had unused ride tickets in my pocket? But, what do I do with my old ideas of obligation? What about the concrete beliefs I grew up with, the ones that had come to define me as a person?

I realized that afternoon that I was stuck. I didn't want to be stuck; I wanted to grow. To do that, I saw that I would have to change not *what* I thought about things, but *how* I thought about things. I had to discover valid, new paradigms that would allow me to see truth not from just one viewpoint, but from as many viewpoints as possible.

I remember another afternoon, years later, again in San Francisco when I, as a sea captain, came ashore to have lunch with an attorney friend. He invited his accountant, a pleasant man I had met before, to come along. During lunch the accountant plied me with questions, "Have you ever seen a whale jump? Did you ever swim with a shark? What is a wild sea like at night?" He couldn't get enough of my stories.

I walked them back to their office and said good-bye. But as I was leaving the office, this curious man called out to me; "Say, Bob, do me a favor will you? When you're out on that sea, surrounded by dolphins and sunsets, think of this sailor, locked up in the body of an accountant!" The people around us laughed, but I did not laugh and neither did he. He meant it.

I, too, had been locked in my identity before the day Leon died. But, on that day I set myself free. That accountant's story has stayed with me for years and I still wonder if he ever broke free. Or had his life, like a leaky faucet, continued trickling away his passion and purpose for living until at the end, he would look back and realize he had made a mistake.

When I was a boy, we were quite poor. Yet, in nearly every housing project that we lived, there was a library where I could get books that allowed me to escape to other times and places. As I read of the adventurers in those books, I made a list of what I wanted to do when I grew up; sea captain, wilderness guide, scuba-diving instructor, commercial fisherman, forester, firefighter, ambulance attendant, explorer, singer, comedian, actor and writer. My mom said I could never do them all, that I had to settle down and focus on one thing. My grandmother accused me of being arrogant and foolish for wanting such glory for myself. As my list grew and adults told me my dreams were fantasies, I became more and more despondent. Life didn't seem worth living if I had to live it in that box. I was a kid from a housing project, with no father and with brothers and sisters to support. I felt like I was in a cage looking out at all those who were free. When I thought of how impossible my dreams were, I felt like I was dying inside. It wasn't until I was in my mid twenties that I suddenly realized I had already experienced several of the dreams I had written down: I had already been a firefighter, forester, commercial fisherman and truck driver. Slowly, my goals were actually being accomplished.

I have heard of others who made similar lists and were also amazed to find they were accomplishing their dreams. But by the time I met Leon, I had been bogged down with obligations. I wanted to quit and go follow my dreams, but I could hear my grandma's voice telling me; "See there, you just cannot keep a job, can you? You start getting ahead and then you quit and go start over somewhere else. You'll never amount to anything!" Every time I wanted to go off to another adventure, I felt the shame in my grandma's voice. But eventually I went anyway, the calling was just too strong to ignore.

Working in medical emergencies initially fulfilled a craving inside me, but the craving had been fulfilled and still I had not moved on. I kept thinking I had to discipline myself so I might "amount to something." I had given up my dreams and taken my place in harness alongside the other prisoners, who had also traded the sacredness of their lives for the security of sameness. In trying to please the voice in my head, I stuck with a safe job, avoiding situations and ideas that might lead me astray. I was missing my life!

Each of us is born with the opportunity to fly to our farthest dreams and beyond. We are blessed with both the abilities and the passion for that journey. The gift of being able to do whatever we can dream of is so valuable and unique it is hard to believe we would discard it. But most of us do because they are gifts that, unlike titles or paychecks, cannot be measured and quantified. Our dreams do not fit nicely into the boxes of other's imaginations. We have to risk being different and we won't ever get approval for being different, unless it makes us famous. Instead, we will suffer disapproval and outright rejection. We must each fight and struggle against the resistance of others if we are to put our own patches into the quilt of history. People will dissuade us from being who we are because our independence may be threatening to them. Plus, there is no question that following one's life mission is difficult and that the battles often leave scars. However, because every day will be filled with grace, the quest will be worth every heartache and every frustration. Perhaps, the greatest thrill we can experience will be at the end of this life, looking back with a smile and saying: "Yes! I did it! I am now completely fulfilled!"

The other option is to live with our lights dimmed way down, letting others decide what is good for us, watching life's true purposes and rewards slip away. For many it is easier to just let their fears paralyze them. But fear is not supposed to paralyze, it is supposed to motivate, that is why it is given to us; as an energizer.

Jane's Story

In a seminar, I met Jane Marcus; a single, thirty-six year-old office manager, who had, for as long as she could remember, felt unfulfilled, alone and slightly out of balance with the Universe. Jane had tried various ways of filling the emptiness within her; food, sex, books and fine, old wines. But none of them had worked. Every distraction became a thinner and thinner veil she tried to hide behind. And always, the emptiness came back.

"Sure, I feel a little disconnected," she once told me in counseling. "Doesn't everyone? I think you just have to put on a happy face and go forward."

"But do you feel that you're doing what you came here to do?"

"What do you mean?"

"If you were to die tomorrow, would you have any regrets?"

"Sure, who wouldn't? No one wants to die."

Jane didn't get it; she thought I asked if she would regret dying; not whether she would regret not having lived. She just wasn't ready to see that yet. She thought her feeling of being disconnected (and I think that's a perfect description) was a natural condition. But it isn't natural to feel disconnected, unless you are disconnected. When we are doing our life's work, we can't feel disconnected because the Universe (Great Spirit) floods us with excitement and the people and resources needed to help us in doing our life's work. That empty, lost feeling is Great Spirit's way of getting our attention. It is saying: "Hey, pay attention! You're on a special mission here with things you're supposed to be experiencing and things you are supposed to be creating! Your time is running, quit stalling and get moving!"

We each have unique gifts and places to apply them. And we'll never feel completely right until we find those gifts and wake them up and let them lead us into our life's missions.

If I were writing Jane's story as a children's book, I would tell of a beautiful high-speed passenger train named Jane, born in a freight yard, among freight trains, not knowing who she is, spending her life feeling out of place, hauling pig iron in her lovely passenger compartments and chugging everyday from one yard to another. Then, one day, she would see a train like herself streaming across the horizon and, at that moment, discover her true nature. Then would come the birth of passion and, of course, she'd have to go through the pain of changing her identity, fighting her way out of the freight yard, suffering the mockery of her old friends. Finally the book would end with Jane the train, clean, shiny and smiling, doing a hundred fifty miles an hour through the countryside, filled with happy people. She would at last be doing her life's work.

There were only two things stopping Jane from living free. First, she didn't understand her specialness and uniqueness. Second, she was fearful of changing her old accepted patterns. She'd worked hard to establish her comfort zone and even though she still felt incomplete, she figured that is just the way life is. She said, "Eventually, you have to quit fighting and learn to live with it."

"What is your mission?" I asked. "What about what you came here to do? Don't you feel something missing in your life? Have you been ignoring your mission for so long that you don't feel it anymore?"

"What mission?" she laughed, "Do you really believe we each have a mission? If I had a mission, I think I'd know it! Look, we're just here to grab what's available and try to be happy with it. And then we die. That's it, okay? What else is there? "

It would be hard to convince Jane because I know it's not easy finding one's mission, one's special life's work. But think of this: just searching for it is the first part of the mission itself! I remember when my mission was a great heap of colored yarn inside me, crying to be woven into a tapestry. I was frustrated and didn't know why or how to get out of it. No one, not you or anyone else, could have looked inside me and said what that tapestry would be like. It was my mission to pull that yarn, yard by yard, out of my heart and weave it into something that felt good and valuable. When you simply cannot not take a step because you don't know where that step will lead you, you must go forward in the trust that you are not alone, that you are being guided by a homing beacon inside you, a divine inspiration that will lead you where you need to go. This is your soul's song, and you need to listen. You can't know what your tapestry will look like before you start to weave, which is the reason most people never start; they want a career counselor to tell them the end of the book before it's written.

You must trust your soul. If you have lost touch with that self, the one you knew so well as a child, then you need to awaken it. How? In this book, I will lay out some patterns for you. If you follow them, your dreams will awaken and begin to pull you along in the direction of your soul. You then will be who you have dreamed of being. Thoreau tells us to: "*Go confidently in the direction of your dreams. Live the life you have imagined.*" It doesn't matter how far-fetched the dream may seem now. You will eventually make it come true; you really will! The difference between successful and non-successful people is that successful people do more than just dream. They go confidentially in the direction of their dreams. Just imagine being Leon Ames, coming to the end of his life and suddenly realizing he *could* have done it!

But perhaps, now you are wondering: how do I find my life's mission, my path? There are two ways; the first is through the logical steps outlined in the following pages, that is the easiest and most secure. The second is what I call the catastrophic method. I used this method for most of my young life. It was like being in a large, completely darkened building, unable to see at all. I needed to find the door, so I ran at full speed until I hit something, most often the wall. Then I would get over my disappointment, and take off running again. Occasionally I hit the door and it was great! I didn't know about the music of my soul, or how to listen to it. When I first met her, it was this catastrophic method that Jane had been following.

The more I worked with her, the more I came to understand Jane's problem. Her father was a visionary and a risk-taker; always beaming with excitement, always looking for new adventures and experiences.

He often failed, but he also had some wonderful victories. He talked to her when she was young, always asking; "What are your dreams and what are your ideas about this or that? She delighted him because her mind was full of treasures, things she imagined that no one else wanted to hear about. Together they investigated possibilities of what she might someday be. She told her dad her dreams of being an artist, an actress, an author, and of ideas she had of creating new inventions. No matter how far-fetched her visions seemed, he carefully listened and encouraged her. But as she grew older, she felt the pressures of "normal" attitudes about life and gradually became uneasy with the insecurity of her dreams. She decided that they were, after all, just fantasies. She wanted something safe, something secure. After college, she found herself avoiding those deep conversations with her dad. She kept things light; too light and eventually began avoiding him; she couldn't bear the disappointment in his eyes.

Where is the safety inside prison walls? Is a trapped bird safe? Our safety does not come from imprisoning ourselves; it comes from building our confidence and courage and learning to fly higher and higher. If we realized we are eternal souls, here on individual divine missions, we will begin to expand in wisdom and personal power and find then, the greatest security is being one with the Universe. When we ignore our souls, we do so at great risk. When we refuse to leave the safety of what we know, and grow beyond our horizons, we shut off the flow of grace. Then things get tough and we have even more of a tendency to hide and play it safe. But, hiding does not help; without the blessings of our souls we swim against the current of life where everything is hard and every success has to be hammered out with desperation.

Some of us may not wake up in this incarnation; may not see the Light until the day we die. Until then, we may walk lock-step behind the one in front of us, careful to not appear different. When Jane did wake up; it was on the bottom of a freezing river in mid-winter.

She had been boating with friends and sat on the boat's railing as it came alongside the dock. Her friends were all looking away from her, watching the docking procedure when the boat suddenly lurched and she toppled over backward. No one saw her go; no one heard the splash. The current dragged her under the boat in water so cold her head felt like daggers were stabbing through it. Her chest clamped tight and she felt her heart struggling against the cold. She did not give up easily and tried to swim; but, the current was too strong. It pulled her deeper, deeper until her ears were screaming with pain. Then Jane knew she was about to die.

She never expected to die like this; nor so young. Yet, here she was, being swept along a river bottom watching all her well-built walls of security dissolve. Her fear paralyzed her. Even greater than her fear of dying was the sadness of knowing she was about to lose her life and had not yet lived it. She had almost never been totally intoxicated with joy. She'd never followed her mission long enough for it to teach her who she was. She had played it safe.

Because she was now flowing along at the exact speed of the water, Jane didn't feel its motion. It was as though she was floating in one place while the river bottom streamed by her. She grew numb. She forced herself to open her eyes, and was surprised to find that the water was clear. As the river bottom flew past, she saw a big rock flying toward her. Just as she was about to crash into it, the current swept her right around it. Though cold and in pain, Jane couldn't help but be surprised and encouraged. If she missed that rock, then maybe it wasn't over yet. That happenstance inspired her; maybe she could still make it! Her mind slowed as she slipped toward semi-consciousness, while at the same time her soul seemed to be awakening from a long sleep. She had no idea how long she had been underwater, or how long she had been holding her breath, but, it seemed like a long time. A new awareness stirred within her and suddenly, with her eyes wide open, she very much wanted to live.

Her dad's face came to her. She hadn't thought of him for years. The last time she heard from him he was living somewhere down in Florida. What would he do right now? No question, he'd be enjoying every second of this, even if it meant he was dying. She felt hollow inside where he used to live, and her emptiness ached for him. The thirty seconds or so that she had been in the river was all the time she needed to realize that she had been sleep-walking through life. Out of her soul grew a solid determination to live. No longer afraid, she felt angry and it felt good. Her anger gave her courage and her courage became determination. She could not swim with her heavy, waterlogged overcoat pulling at her. She ripped it off and immediately felt the knives of icy water biting into her. It didn't matter now. She reached up, kicking and pulling for the surface, her lungs bursting for air. A fisherman on the shore thought he heard an otter splashing the surface. Then he saw her face, almost blue.

Later, in the hospital, the doctors told her she'd nearly died of hypothermia. "I really did die!" she told me later, "I'm not the same person who fell off that boat." At the age of thirty-six, Jane discovered the wonderful opportunity of living fully and then began her life's work. She had finally been born.

Richard, a friend of mine, went through school, became a lawyer, and had a good practice for several years. But something wasn't right; something was unfinished, unfulfilled within him. He found himself becoming fascinated with architecture. So, he went back college and got a degree in architecture. He then had a flourishing career as an architect and loved the work. But after a few years, that light also began to dim and he became restless; his soul called him. What am I talking about when I say your soul? More accurately I should say; "you-as-soul." Because, you are it; you don't have it. When we are in grace, we can feel it pulling at us. Richard went to his architect office every day, but his soul tugged at his mind and body like a kite in the wind. Instead of doing what most of us do, which is to wind in the string so we no longer feel the pull, Richard followed his soul's call. He went to medical school and became a pediatrician.

Knowing him, this may not be the end; his next job may be in Real Estate or in nuclear physics. Richard is dedicated to living his life fully and he will go wherever his soul directs him. Following one's soul is much like following a child picking flowers in a meadow; the child may want flowers from the *entire* meadow in the bouquet instead of just staying with daisies. I'm sure there are those who think Richard failed as an attorney and as an architect too, because, like my dear grandma, they see us as failures when we abandon our security for our dreams.

When I was a thirty-four years old, I was a hardworking sea captain who had once again forgotten my mission. I was so focused on my routines and adventures, I was not paying attention to the fact that I had done what I came to do and it was time to move on. So I was blown out of my mental hiding place by a killer hurricane. Afterward I realized that for several years I had been out of grace and fighting against the spiritual current, driven by obligation rather than opportunity, doing what I thought I should, rather than listening to what my soul hungered for. I took my life back on that crazy day, started a new career, and began listening to my soul again. I found myself speaking before audiences, and realized I had things to say that made a difference in their lives. It was a wonderful revelation. I became a writer and lecturer and eventually spread my teachings over a few hundred thousand people in fifteen countries. If it were not for the hurricane, I might still be dulling my wits on a job that no longer challenged me. Now I am also a Realtor. I have no idea what other hats I may yet wear in this lifetime. I'm listening to my soul and am willing to risk following whenever it calls me. I feel blessed because I realize that miracles have always happened just when I need them. Think now, isn't the same true for you? If you were willing to follow your soul's calling, would you ever go wrong?

"Its okay, Grandma; I'm letting my soul lead in this dance, and it is good."

The Soul's Mission: Experience and Express!

Growth is synonymous with life; all living things are either growing or they are dying. We grow by *experiencing* fresh adventures and *expressing* those experiences. Every new experience, when expressed, makes us wiser, deeper, and more in tune with Great Spirit; this is what our Souls brought us here for—it is how they grow.

Here's how it works: We inhale a new experience and our wisdom is expanded by it. Then we express that experience and the wisdom becomes permanent. It is this wisdom that teaches us who we are. A native in the Amazon jungle sees a great snake and kills it. He has experienced something outside his comfort zone, his normal routine. He expresses his adventure to the tribe that night in dance or song or however he chooses, and his identity is forever expanded in his eyes and the eyes of others. If he had not expressed his experience, the event would have eventually faded and he would have gained little from it. We express our experiences, our wisdom expands, and we see life anew; we become enchanted by the realization of possibilities we'd never dreamed of. We will never be the same.

Take A Risk!

The only way to have a *new* experience is to risk; to venture beyond the safety of our established comfort zones to places we've never been before; to be swept through new adventures and self-discoveries as Jane was swept along the river bottom.

In my years around boats, I have always been amazed at the numbers of vessels that never leave the dock. Marinas are full of waiting, unused boats. The boat-builder intended them to cut through the waves and ride the wind, carrying people into the unknown. But most of them sit year after year, gathering moss and dust, until they are scrapped without having ever discovered their potentials. Many of us are just like those boats, scared to leave our safe harbors and sail into the open sea, into situations we cannot predict, afraid the open sea will swallow us. If only we knew how well our Builder had designed each of us to follow our dreams, we'd trust our seaworthiness. But how will we ever learn that trust if we don't take some initial risks? How will we discover the wonderful adventures waiting just beyond the breakwater?

If we start with a few easy risks and see that we can win, our confidence will grow, our comfort zones expand and our fears turn into excitement. Then, because excitement and personal growth are addictive, we will be hooked; looking for every opportunity to cast off and head into the sea of new experiences.

Here is how to begin: Find a vision, something that, if accomplished will give you a feeling of fulfillment. It need not be a big thing, going to see a friend, taking a hike, making a resume, losing five pounds, whatever it is just set your sights on it. Then every day, take one step outside of your comfort zone toward that vision; one step, no matter how small. If you will set and accomplish that one small goal outside your comfort zone today, you can declare that you have won the day. If you will do that for at least four days of this week, you can declare that you have won the week. If you do that for three of the weeks this month, you can declare you have won the month. The feeling of power and confidence that will come from that process will amaze you because you will have started along the path of romancing your soul and fulfilling your life's mission. You will know it in every fiber of your being; you will be living on purpose! Just imagine the increased self-confidence, the clarity you will gain and the visions you thought unattainable suddenly coming within reach. Imagine every day saying, "I won this day!" When you are saying this most days, surely you see how completely your life will change.

A risk is not the same thing as a gamble; with gambling, you can really lose; money, your car, even your home. But, with risk taking, you are *guaranteed* to gain. What is the difference between risk taking and gambling? Research scientists are risk takers, not gamblers; they attempt to find cures for diseases and they fail at the task hundreds of times, yet they are winning with every single failure because they are learning and getting closer to the one experiment that will finally reveal the truth to them—the cure. They know they will eventually find it and it will make every failure valuable. But gamblers do not win with every loss, and there is no end result that will justify their losses. A boy who dives off a bridge not knowing what is under the water is gambling, if he misses the logs and rocks he wins. If he hits one he loses and the game is over. His loss does not lead to eventual victory. Our souls do not ask us to gamble, they ask us to trust the light within us and the grace around us, to trust that we are here on divine missions and that we will be guided past the rocks into fulfilling our life's work. When we are following our souls, every failure gets us closer to our dreams. By starting in the wrong direction, we discover the right direction, by making mistakes we learn; its all part of the process. But nothing new or different can ever happen to us until we decide to make new and different choices.

The Blessing of Fear

Pure energy. That's all fear is. Fear has no intelligence, so it can't, as so many teachers and philosophers have suggested, be evil; it is simply energy. Like any energy—dynamite, gasoline, fire or water— it can either serve or destroy. If allowed to, it can paralyze us. When harnessed to our dreams, it is converted into *usable* energy, into *excitement.* It empowers us. That is the Creator's intention for fear; that it motivate and strengthen us. Every great innovation and every great victory since the beginning of mankind was accomplished through the help of fear energy. Did you grow up as I did, fearing fear? Did you avoid things that were scary? Oh yes, there are truly dangerous things that should be avoided; but I'm not talking about those. I'm talking about things like being honest in relationships, speaking in front of a crowd, taking a new job or registering for school, displaying your creative abilities for all to see; standing by your ethics when people about you are abandoning theirs. Those are the kinds of fears I'm talking about. When something in your soul calls you to move and you say "yes," the Universe supplies you with the fuel to accomplish it. This is the fear—the pure energy—that raises us up to the next level and accomplish our soul's dreams.

Fear walks hand in hand with growth opportunity—always. This morning I was sleeping soundly and suddenly was awakened by a sound or a dream. My heart hammered; my mind, a few moments ago in dreamland, snapped fully awake and sharp. I listened . . . not a sound. No one had broken into the house; my wife and daughter were sleeping soundly. Yet, I could not go back to sleep. Still afraid, I realized I had enough energy to knock out a chapter in this book. So, even though it is now four in the morning, I'm here writing this message to you and I'm excited about it. I'm energized and motivated by my fear. How did I do that? How did I prevent it from becoming dread or anxiety? I could have lain in my pool of dark fantasies and become convinced I am too small to take risks, but instead I focused that energy into this work.

But what about my sleep? Well, there's the risk; maybe I'll be flat later this afternoon and then I'll have to figure how to handle that. But surely I'll survive. Is the trade off worth it? Would I trade this chapter for three hours of sleep? No way! My missed sleep will soon be forgotten, but hopefully this chapter will live for a long time.

Please remember this—whenever we are afraid, opportunity is at hand! If we recognize the opportunity (which is easy to do when on our missions) we can quickly convert our fear energy into excitement and use it to do something bigger than we thought we could. All fear is convertible to excitement and must be if it is not to default into panic, anxiety or dread. Those are dangerous states to be in because they paralyze us. Like a gasoline hose out of control, unfocused fear spews its volatile energy against us instead of for us. Then it takes over our day and makes our decisions for us, and we lose the day. We simply cannot afford to do that, we must take the raw product of fear and refine it into an energy that will serve us. Then, we can welcome fear as something as natural and as important to our lives as sunshine; a gift without which our lives would be flat, empty, and very short.

Follow Your Passion!

A main characteristic of most successful people is this: *They are led by the passion of their souls.* Their motivation comes from a healthy balance of both opportunity and obligation. We need both. The work of those motivated by solely by obligation is without grace while the work of those motivated solely by opportunity is without value. When I speak of obligation here, I mean this: *The only obligation you have in any lifetime is to be true to your soul.* But how can we do that unless we can hear its calling? (Latin: *vocare*, which means *to call*; hence, *vocation—life's work.*) We learn to recognize its voice by listening to our bliss, our passion; finding that which fulfills our souls. As the late Joseph Campbell told us, we must be following our bliss, our passion, in order to fulfill our lives.

In the Olympic Games of 1988 in Seoul, Korea, an American named Greg Louganis climbed up the ladder to the three meter diving platform and prepared himself for the tenth dive of this competition, knowing that this dive could either move him toward a Gold Medal or eliminate him from competition. It would be the most difficult dive of his career because on his previous dive, only minutes before, his head smashed into the board, ripping open his scalp and knocking him nearly unconscious. His scalp had been sewn up quickly and a waterproof patch applied, then with head throbbing and the image of his mistake tugging at him, he climbed the ladder and readied himself for a dive that would be more difficult and potentially dangerous than the one that just injured him.

How could Greg Louganis or any of us in this condition focus on such a dangerous and precise venture? The competition was so fierce he would need almost a perfect score by the judges. He would need to maintain absolute self-control, perfect flexibility, and precise accuracy. In order to accomplish his mission, he must keep his mind still and his fear channeled into pure energy. In order to pull off this very difficult feat, Louganis must be flowing with grace and with the joy of being alive, of being here at this crucial moment. It is the only way his self-doubts could have been overcome and his fear converted to usable, rather than paralyzing, energy.

Greg Louganis focused on the performance before him, envisioning every turn and movement he would make while falling through the air, fully knowing that no dive he had ever made would require as much of him. He knew he had to be perfect. How could he have such self-confidence? How does one get to such a place of confidence and mastery? It came to him through facing and overcoming challenges and winning the day, every day for years; through this process Louganis had come to understand the power of his soul.

High above the Olympic pool, Louganis walked to the end of the board, knowing he was being watched around the world. He folded his hands in prayerful concentration and paused. Then he jumped and flew high over the watching crowd to perform the exact, graceful, aerial ballet he had envisioned, bringing tears to the millions of eyes of those who were watching breathlessly. His dive was so nearly perfect it allowed him to go forward in the competition, where he made two even more difficult dives, and then went on to win not only his third, but also his fourth Olympic Gold Medal.

We can think of Greg Louganis; "Yes, but he's special, and he has things going for him that I don't." But that would not be true. While it is true that Louganis fought his way through a difficult childhood and that he went to those Olympics with his haunting secret of being HIV positive; he was born with neither more courage nor more opportunities than you or me. An adopted child, he grew up feeling mostly isolated and misunderstood. He was labeled a sissy and called a nigger by schoolmates because of his dark skin. He was beaten by bullies and lived in fear of his adopted father. His great self-confidence did not come to him easily; he earned it through years of proving to himself that he could accomplish what he dreamed of. He did it as we all must, step by step. It is the only way any of us can become our very best. Though diving was Louganis's chosen craft, it is also in each of us to win just as gloriously at our individual missions as he did. Louganis cultivated the tools of success that, in turn, gave him his dreams. It is because he took the time and effort to build those strengths that four Olympic Gold Medals now hang on his wall. If we build those same qualities, we also will attain our own dreams. It is not complicated and it takes no more time to build such tools of strength than it does to practice failing.

At the height of her career, in concert after concert, famous singer, Carly Simon was often numbed by stage fright and yet her performances were always spectacular. How could that be, unless her feelings were being converted from paralyzing anxiety into motivating excitement when she was before her audiences; excitement which allowed her to open her soul and freely express her passion? Like Greg Louganis, Carly Simon had tremendous fears, but through courage and determination she had learned to make them into tremendous personal power. How did she do it? Like all heroes and heroines who have risen above their qualms, she did not let fear make her decisions for her. Her commitment to herself, to her music and her audience were more important than the clawing feeling inside her. No one can do that for us; only we can train that feeling of impending disaster to serve instead of destroy us. We do so by realizing that, *we are not our fears*. We listen to the callings of our souls, then train our minds to automatically change fear into excitement and energize our missions.

Once we have harnessed our fears, we must have a place to focus that energy. We must have goals and visions and a life-mission to accomplish. For some the choice will be to keep things as they are. However if that is not you: if you see your life as an exciting adventure and are ready for the next exciting episode, read on!

A polite, shy woman in one of my seminars admitted that her husband had been abusing her. She said she simply could not leave him. For her that idea was just too scary; and as bad as he was, she didn't want to lose him. Her life was miserable and she lived in constant paralysis and shame. When I asked her if she would leave him if it meant saving her daughter, she seemed to wake up. "Well, of course, if it was my daughter he was beating, I'd be gone today." When I pointed out that she and her husband were systematically training her daughter to marry a man just like her father, who would feel free to abuse her, the woman sat up straight; her confusion and indecision evaporated; she had discovered something more important than her fear. She made the commitment to talk to a counselor at a woman's shelter. That's what I mean by being committed to your goal. If there is nothing to win by working through your fear, why do it?

Step one then, in converting fear to excitement is being committed to something that is more important to you than giving in to your fear. *Step two* is making a plan that will carry you to success. *Trask's Triangle* can simplify that plan. It is an easy to use chart that is working for thousands of people around the world. It will take you step by step through the process of building self confidence by winning the day, every day. Then when we are experiencing what might have once been debilitating fear, we can feel excited, because we have a plan that we know will work.

Babe Ruth went from being the fat little orphan, a butt of jokes among neighborhood kids, to becoming America's darling. Young

George Herman Ruth, abandoned as a child, grew up with constant rejection. Did he have fears like the rest of us? Surely, he had at least as many or more. What happened to those fears? They never went away, but the Bambino learned how to convert them into usable energy. When we have fear, there always must be something that is more important. For Babe it was his passion for baseball. Combined with the energy of fear he made a mark that history will never erase.

We must be committed. When I use the word commitment, I mean determination. When we are *absolutely determined* to use all the energies available to reach our visions we simply cannot fail! With that kind of commitment, nothing can stop us. Mother Teresa, a humble and sometimes feisty nun, spent her life teaching people to love one another while being almost constantly impeded by financial problems, politicians, the Church and mobsters. Constantly being told she couldn't do what she wanted; she did it anyway. Her determination directed her energies to sure success, just as did the determination of Louganis, Simon and Ruth and every other great accomplisher in history.

President Franklin Roosevelt reminded us that: "The only thing we have to fear is fear itself." These other great thinkers echoed his assertion:

Thoreau: "Nothing is so much to be feared as fear."

Wellington: "The only thing I'm afraid of is fear."

Francis Bacon: "Nothing is terrible except fear itself."

Montaigne: "The thing I fear most is fear."

Mark Twain: "Courage is mastery of fear—not absence of fear."

These world-movers were successful and powerful agents of change in their own lives because they clarified what was important to them and then determinedly followed the passions of their souls.

As a little boy I was terrified of deep water. In the pool I carefully worked my way around a swimming pool hanging onto the splash-trough and while my cousin Gary, cavorted out in the middle. He knew I could swim as well as he in shallow water, but I was afraid to be in water over my head. One day, as I walked by the edge of the deep end, he suddenly pushed me in. I thought I would die; but as I swam for the side, I realized how buoyant I was in deeper water. I'm not advo-cating pushing fearful people into deep water, but Gary knew me well and knew it was not my inability but my fear that had me paralyzed. I never again held onto the edge and surely could never have become a SCUBA instructor or a free-diver if Gary had not risked my wrath and helped me move through my fear. We each have our own edges we hang on to. They may be jobs that numb our senses, relationships that tear at our hearts or traumatic memories that convince us we are powerless. Life is meant to be *lived*, not just tolerated. But to live it we have to move out into the pool.

Have you noticed that trees and plants are constantly reaching for the light? If you turn your house plant away from the window, it will turn itself back toward the window. If a tree is crumpled to the forest floor by another falling tree, its top will reach around the fallen trunk and move back up toward the light. All living things grow by reaching for light, whether it is the light of the sun, the light of love, or spiritual light. The urge to grow toward Light is natural, and its attraction pulls us constantly; reluctantly or willingly; along a path of our individual enlightenment.

Change is one of the most frightening things we will ever experi-ence because every change is an ego death. Our egos will torment us with doubt, confusion and terror in order to protect themselves. But what if you convince your ego that you are not trying to change your identity, but instead are going to expand it? Then; rather than losing who I am, I am becoming more.

When I take on a new career, I do not abandon the identities of those of my past. I include them in my evolving identity. At each point of change there is fear, moving from a life in which I felt secure, to one I knew nothing about. I start at the bottom and wonder if I will be successful. I have learned through many life changes that it is okay to be afraid, that fear is the natural feeling that comes to us when we change. It comes just when we need that additional energy. Each time I start a new career, I feel like a butterfly coming out of my cocoon. It's one of the most exciting times of my life because I feel a new me being born. When I keep showing up and saying "yes", my soul, like the kite in the wind, keeps pulling me over new horizons. Thousands of us are winning at life because we sail out of our safe harbors and trust that we can handle the wide and wild sea of life. We know we weren't built to sit at the dock; we belong at sea, challenging the storms and living our lives fully while the opportunity is still here.

Let me finish this chapter by returning to the Leon Ames story— As he lay dying, dear Leon changed my life with his precious words, and through me he has then changed the lives of many thousands more. He was crushed when he realized his mistake; that he had not followed his soul's urging, and that as a result he was dying having truly missed the boat. As I write these words I remember clearly how his sorrow affected me on that gray, wet afternoon.

Thank you, Leon! As you can see; we're building our boats now.

CHAPTER TWO

IT'S NEVER TOO LATE TO GROW

◇◇◇◇◇◇◇

Three Ways of Living: Be, Do and Have

There is no question in my mind that you are a special person. There has never been, nor will there ever be another you. No one will ever have a replica of your fingerprints, your cell structure, your personality or your viewpoint of reality. No one will ever accomplish what you can. Until you are walking the exact path you came here to travel, your life cannot help but feel unfulfilled. How does a person do that? How do you find your path, your individual mission?

I was watching a pitching duel between a great pitcher and a great batter recently. With the count three balls and two strikes, the batting champion fouled away pitch after pitch. Soon there were no more surprises; the batter had seen everything the pitcher had and the pitcher had seen everything the batter had. The pressure on each of them was tremendous. The announcer said it all: "Ladies and gentlemen, this is no longer a baseball game; this is now a head game." A head game, wow! He was saying that the game was about much more than baseball. It was about how the pitcher and batter each saw himself, about which had the greater self-confidence and was the most balanced. It was about which could hold the vision of himself more clearly as the winner of the contest. After fouling off pitch after pitch, finally the pitcher just threw a fast ball down the center of the plate, so fast the batter was caught off-guard and could not catch up with it. The pitcher won.

We are also in the head game. It is your mental and emotional strength that will determine whether you win or lose at relationships, money, health and career. In order to have the strength, our *being*, *doing*, and *having* must be balanced.

Living well is like riding a bicycle; nearly impossible to stay balanced unless we are in motion, but the motion of our lives must flow between these three poles equally. I'll use Melvin, Patricia, and Larry as examples to illustrate what happens when we get out of balance. We'll call Melvin a human *having*, because he is focused on what he has: money, cars, houses, and toys. He still feels empty and knows there must be something more, but having is the only way he knows of fulfilling himself. He keeps accumulating "things" hoping one of them will bring him joy.

Patricia is our human *doing*. She can't stop working; she is busy from the time she wakes up in the morning until she drops off to

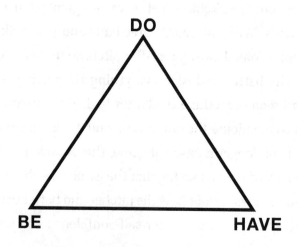

sleep at night, thoroughly exhausted. She doesn't have time to just *be* in her world or to enjoy *having* anything. Like Melvin, she knows something is missing, but is convinced that the only way to fill the void is to work harder.

Larry is our human *being*; he meditates, talks endlessly about spiritual and metaphysical stuff, but he *does* little to challenge himself and *has* very little to show for it. He is self-indulgent, isolated, and his life is stagnant. Larry knows something's not quite right, so he digs deeper into spiritual philosophies and meditates more.

If these three were following their souls they would not be lost because the food of the soul is joy. If they do not feel joy, the soul will pull them in the direction to where they can feel joy. Neither Melvin, Patricia, nor Larry is finding joy because none of them are in balance. They are in avoidance of what they do not understand and unwilling to risk learning it. In order to know joy and to be operating at the top of our game, we must stay balanced in *being, doing*, and *having*. When those three are in harmony, our souls are smiling and avenues of opportunity open before us. Where we only saw problems, we now see possibilities, and are able to achieve things we never thought we could.

Jane, who was reborn on the bottom of the river, never heard of Be-Do-Have. After her ordeal she determined to keep moving forward, feeding her soul the pure joy which naturally flows from a balanced life. In Figure 2 we see what she learned.

As you can see in Figure 2 (next page), at **BE**, we Rest. At **DO**, we Change. At **HAVE**, we Win. Between Rest and Change is the action path of Discovery. Between Change and Win is the action path of Risk. Between Win and Rest is the action path of Self-Love. As our visions pull us forward into a sea of unlimited opportunity, we will find excitement and adventure and will accomplish all we can dream

of. But it is not automatic; we are still encountering CHOICE at every corner. Fear, all around the outside of the Triangle, is our motivator. If we are afraid of fear, then at Rest, we choose Avoidance, at Change we choose Anxiety, at Win we choose Unworthiness. We often make those strange choices because we have been taught that fear is our enemy and that we should avoid fear if at all possible. We can make simple choices at these three corners of the Triangle and our lives will suddenly feel empowered and will take on new meaning.

All that is required to change our minds about fear is to see fear as pure energy. We will need that energy to clarify our thinking about our visions and missions and to keep moving forward when we have doubts. When we stay on the outside of the Triangle, we grow. When we go inside, our growth stops; we become weak and confused. Victors live on the outside, victims live inside. We choose every day to either be creators or casualties; to either take progressive steps or to crawl inside and allow our self-worth and confidence to erode. Some people spend their entire lives inside the Triangle, not realizing that at any moment they could change their lives completely. If you decide to live on the outside, the first thing you will need is determination, especially if you have a history of being victimized by life. The longer you have lived your life as a victim the harder it will be to change; but you can do it, you can become the creator of your own reality. At this moment all you need to do is decide whether you are going to live a proactive or a reactive life. Every single day from now on can be better than the day before when you use the Triangle.

	Proactive Growth Form	Reactive Stagnant Form
BEING	Resting	Avoidance
DOING	Changing	Anxiety
HAVING	Winning	Unworthiness

It is well documented that fun is important to productivity. Corporations that make work fun for employees are by far the most successful. Athletes who never forget they are playing a game are the best players. Parents who laugh with their kids keep them around to watch them grow. When we're not having fun, we get off track. Stress destroys our creative efforts; we lose the ability to see the light and to create with magic; we have fallen from grace with our souls. In order to be proactive, we must stay in joy as much as possible. Remember, joy is the food of the soul; if we want to harness our soul's power, we must feed it. When we are laughing at our mistakes, forgiving others and flowing with life, the windows of our souls open and anything is possible. When we are unhappy our ego's defenses take charge and change becomes difficult.

Darla, one of my students, parachuted from a plane for fun. A week later she jumped again, twice. She loved it and it was easy to see she had been changed by the process. But then she surprised me by saying she wasn't going to jump again. I asked her why. She shrugged; "I've accomplished that, I don't need to keep doing it now. I want to move on to new experiences."

"So what's next, then?" I asked.

She was quiet a minute. Then she said, "Well, now it's time to deal with my marriage, which I've been avoiding because it is a lot scarier than jumping out of a plane!"

She had discovered the fun of winning, and she was excited about it. She had gained the self-confidence necessary to take the next step in her life.

So Darla asked herself, what do I really want in this relationship? The answer had three parts: what she wanted to be, do, and have with her husband. Using the Triangle made the process easy.

Trask's Triangle not only keeps Be-Do-Have balanced so that our creative power stays energized, but it also gradually changes old, automatic habits—programs that no longer serve us. It takes us, by the shortest route, to the realization of our dreams. Every person who ever accomplished great things did it by using these principles; I've simply taken the lessons of history's greatest successes and put them in a format anyone can use.

By watching our parents and others fail we learn to be failures too. Through the brutal discovery that our success sometimes can lose us friends, we learn that winning can be perilous. Then we develop self-limitations that are more familiar and safer and more compatible with the belief systems of ourselves, our parents and our peers. But self-limitation like this kills your passion for life and leaves you empty. If you have problems with intimate relationships, a constant struggle with money, or a career that doesn't fulfill you, perhaps you are being automatically programmed by your subconscious mind to do what protects the status quo. If so, it is a pattern that can eventually become your comfort zone; and your personal identity and if so, your ego will do anything to keep you from changing it. Because this process works undercover, the only way to realize it is to recognize that the same failing results keep repeating themselves and that whatever you do to create new results is being subconsciously sabotaged. How can we get different results when we keep using those methods that give us what we don't want? We must take charge of our lives and change those subconscious patterns. That is the value of the Triangle.

The purpose of the Triangle path is to lead you, step by step, into creating an identity that empowers you. The steps have been monitored and carefully adjusted over the past twenty-five years through the coaching and feedback of tens of thousands of people. This method of self-empowerment has led countless people to create their dreams; to become successful film stars, authors, athletes, entrepreneurs, and to have fulfilling relationships. They may be successful, but they have had to fight the same inner demons as we do. Expanding their identities to include such enormous success was no doubt very challenging. As we know from the arrests, suicides, drug addictions and broken relationships, many of them are still struggling to accept their new identities. Expanding to new identities, widening our comfort zones is not easy; but it is the most worthwhile work we will do in this lifetime. All you need do is follow the Triangle path until the process of making good choices becomes automatic; then watch as miracles begin to transform your life.

Take another look at the figure on page 36. The journey begins at Rest (**Be**) in the lower left-hand corner, and follows the outside arrows clockwise along a path of Discovery, where we realize and admit what we really want. Once we have that answer, we'll define it into an achievable vision: a goal. At the corner called Change (**Do**), we recognize the following important truth: It is our minds, not the world around us that must change in order for us to have the lives we want. Then from Change we take a Risk, expanding our identities by challenging old patterns that have blocked our dreams. At the Win (**Have**) corner, we validate our progress and anchor our developing new identity. This is where our self-confidence really starts building as we choose the path of *Self-Love*.

At each corner of the Triangle is choice. What if we make the wrong choices? Let's look at what happens: Inside the Triangle, we are pulled along a counterclockwise path into deeper self-doubt and helplessness. Once inside the Triangle we descend toward despair, losing our confidence and becoming more helpless and confused. We are in a flushing toilet spinning around and being sucked deeper into the darkness. If, at the place of Rest, we choose Avoidance over Discovery we will rotate from Avoidance through Boredom into Unworthiness, through Guilt/Shame into Anxiety, through Paralysis and back into Avoidance. Each time we spiral downward we fall farther out of grace and our life force grows weaker. A good thing about the Triangle is that we can see ahead of time what the consequences of our choices will be.

Long misty shafts of light, streaming through the high canopy, splashed down across the dark forest floor where we sat around Tia Maria, watching a tricky blue jay and a feisty gray squirrel locked in battle over a handful of nuts she had thrown to them. The squirrel charged the bird, his tail bobbing furiously; the jay flew up over his head, then dipped to grab a nut and fluttered to a branch to eat it. The squirrel was furious. He gathered as many nuts as he could cram into his cheeks and he dashed back and forth, his angry tail thrashing the air. But each time he started away to bury them, the jay swooped and grabbed another of his treasures. The squirrel was beside himself with frustration: Should he leave the nuts to go bury the ones in his mouth, sacrificing some of those still on the ground to the jay, or stand guard and never get any into his cache?

A young woman named Elizabeth laughed, "That squirrel reminds me of me."

"Why is that?" asked Tia Maria.

"Well, that's how I spend my life, dashing around trying to make the right choices. I'm just like that squirrel, I feel wrong no matter what I do. I'm frustrated; I'm tired of being a squirrel."

"And you have a son, don't you?"

Elizabeth nodded. "His father and I are divorced." She sighed. "Boy, he sure isn't any help!"

The forest was quiet as Tia Maria held the student in her gaze. After a moment, she said, "Are you being fair to yourself?"

Tears appeared in her eyes. "Fair? I don't know. I'm doing the best I can, but still I I'm just falling deeper and deeper into a black hole. I watch my life going by and I'm . . . I'm just missing it." She wiped her eyes on her sleeve. "My son needs me all the time, but I need a life too, don't I?" She looked at Tia Maria. "I feel like I'm trapped."

"You're tired, child."

"Whew, I am! I'm exhausted all the time." She pushed her hair back, "exhausted and lonely."

It was quiet while she dug out her handkerchief and again wiped her eyes. "Oh, maybe I'm just being a victim. Maybe I just expect too much."

"How does your son feel about all this?"

She shrugged, "I wonder if he thinks he's a burden. I get short-tempered with him. I don't mean to, but I just lose it."

"You don't want to live like this, do you?"

"No! But what can I do? I love my son; I need to take care of him. What else can I do?"

Tia Maria smiled. "Do something for me, will you please?"

"Sure!"

"Walk over to that tree."

Elizabeth stood and walked to the tree, and the squirrel fled up its trunk, scolding her in a loud voice. The jay sat on an adjacent branch and watched.

"Now, walk to that one over there."

She did as she was told.

"OK, come on back now and have a seat. Tell me child, how did you do that?"

"Do what? You mean walk around. I just . . . did it."

"Was it hard?"

"No," Elizabeth smiled.

"Confusing?"

"No."

"Did you have a choice?"

"Sure, I could have refused."

"But you chose to do it. It was your choice. You walked from one place to another and it wasn't hard for you. But in your life, child, you can't move like that can you? Because you're emotionally attached to staying in one place."

Elizabeth leaned forward, "But in my life I don't have choices like that."

"But what if you do have choices? Could it be that you have stayed in that helpless place so long, you have come to think it is who you are? Then how can you see anything new? It becomes a habit to think in only one way, and to go around in the same small circles, seeing only

what is familiar. But, my goodness, child, it is only a habit! One you can break. Look at those trees again, it is as easy as moving to them, you just have to be able to see your options through new eyes."

"Okay, yes; that's what I want!"

A beam of light from above flickered about Tia Maria, gleaming in her silver hair as she leaned toward Elizabeth. "Then you'll have to reach outside of yourself to find that new viewpoint. Then you will start making new decisions about yourself and your life. It will be scary, but you can do it. Reach child, until finally you leave behind your identity as a helpless person. You will know when that happens because you will then look back and see your helplessness as only an illusion. Now, it's going to take you thirty days of hard work. Are you willing to do that?"

"I am, yes."

Tia Maria took a stick and began to draw a Triangle on the ground before her.

How often do you feel you need a miracle? Are you making a space for one to happen? Sometimes our despair is the result of our unwillingness to change our identities. Then, like an alcoholic or drug addict, we need to hit bottom; things have to get so bad we simply cannot take it anymore, then we are finally willing to let go of what keeps us trapped. How about Elizabeth, can she rise above her situation? The truth is there is no situation we cannot rise above if we just know how to take command of our lives. Elizabeth can be, do and have anything she wants if she is willing to become the creator of her life, to be proactive instead of reactive.

How many of your dreams seem so far away you only see them as fantasies? What would you like to have in terms of Creativity, Relationships, Wealth, Health or Career? By training your mind to be a powerful creator of your reality, you can have whatever you dare to dream. But when we fall inside the Triangle, we fall from grace; we lose the ability to change our lives. Then we can't see how to make right choices; we are sabotaging our lives without ever realizing it.

Please take a few minutes to again study the figure on page 36. Using Creativity, Relationships, Wealth, Health or Career as areas in which to create dreams, how are you doing? Where do you go inside the Triangle? Is it choosing Avoidance over Discovery? Is it choosing Anxiety over Risk? Or is it choosing Unworthiness over Self-Love? In the past year how often have you made the choices that have sapped your creative power? Can you see that there is a certain comfort in making those choices? I'm asking you now to expand your comfort zone and your identity and practice making new decisions at those vital corners.

The Triangle Is a Spiral

On paper, the Triangle appears flat, one-dimensional, but in truth, each circuit we make around the outside takes us upward, while each circuit around the inside takes us downward. Like hawks on the wind, we may soar in spiraling triangles, wider and higher or descend counterclockwise so that we constantly become weaker and less confident. Some people have made Triangle walks in their gardens, with carved stones or signs to indicate the choice points. Then, when dealing with a confusing situation, they walk it out on the Triangle.

Let's walk around the Triangle together now and see what our choices are. Imagine yourself at rest. Then an idea comes into your mind of something that would be thrilling to accomplish, some-thing that seems beyond your abilities right now. Suggested places to choose from are Relationships, Peace of Mind, Health, Wealth, Career or Adventures you want to experience. If you find yourself resisting this process you have already chosen to go inside the Triangle into Avoidance. But if you have chosen Discovery and come up with a Vision then let's move forward.

CHAPTER THREE

FOLLOWING YOUR SOUL AROUND THE TRIANGLE

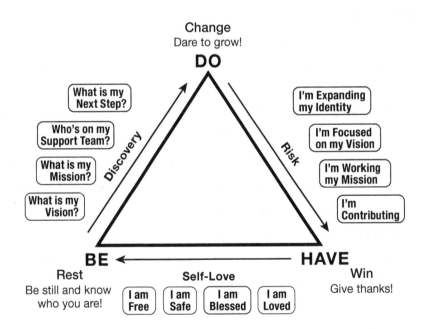

Choose either Discovery or Avoidance

As spiritual beings or souls, we cannot die; we have lived and will live forever. We incarnated into these physical forms in order to experience and express and thereby grow in wisdom and joy. We come for the same reason chess players come to games: to enjoy ourselves and to become better players in the process. The challenge is to do both at the same time; stay in joy and overcome challenges. So if we're not in joy, we're out of grace and our souls are starving; we're not in the game, and we're wasting our time here. If we go through each day feeling oppressed or trapped, we're not following our true life's missions. So the Vision you choose must be exciting to you. You cannot choose because you are obligated or because you "should" make that choice, it has to be one that allows you to be in joy while accomplishing it.

What Is My Vision?

As we move into Discovery, our first step is: *What is my Vision?* This universe is made up of molecules, which are made up of atoms, which in turn are made up of sub-atomic particles. Those particles are made up of energy and information or we could say, intelligent energy. They are vibrations that correlate with the vibration of the Universe and all together they are the Universal consciousness and creative power. We each are vibrations, and our thoughts are vibrations too, very real and powerful ones that go out from us and change the physical nature of the reality around us. This truth has been physically proven in experiments by quantum physicists; your thoughts are affecting the reality around you right now; they are creating the reality you perceive. When you hold a vision—a soul calling, you are sending out a vibration that links you to the reality of that vision in the Creative Universe. By keeping that vision clear and staying committed to it, you are following a line of attraction that will bring your vision into being as surely as if you were driving to it along a paved highway. You're life is blessed and you are flowing with grace.

Our visions should be so sparkling and enchanting that they inspire us, pull us out of ourselves and make us want to grow. Then our fears will become pure energy and empower us to do what we normally could not. Or, we can make another choice and be stuck. We are thus inspired by our visions and motivated by our fears or sabotaged by our guilts and self-doubts. If we allow those guilts and self-doubts to become dominate, they become the "dark stuff" that impedes the flow of grace. It is impossible to reach a vision while dragging behind us our guilt, shame, resentment or regret. But if you make your vision your boss, and allow nothing to come between you and it, you will eventually erase your "dark stuff."

A true vision enchants us, holds our attention and draws us into and along the path of our enlightenment. When an idea or goal is so captivating it causes us to smile and at the same time scares us and causes our creative juices to flow, that's a vision!

How can you know your vision? Here is an example; you are watching TV and get hungry for cherry pie. Where did that come from? Now your mouth's watering; you have a vision of something you truly want. Every vision comes with a mission path to it. If your vision is a cherry pie, and if it is really a vision, not just a fantasy, then here is your mission path: keys ... coat ... car ... bakery ... home ... and yum! With the taste of cherry pie tingling in your mind, you won't get distracted from your mission path.

Any true vision will be just as tantalizing as that cherry pie to your soul. And your life will be made up of lot's of visions, large and small. If you deliberately take the Triangle steps to make the cherry pie visions come true, you will be training yourself for accomplishing the big ones. You must be enjoying the process though, or you fall from grace. Remember the food of the soul is joy.

The clue to finding a vision is this: what excites you? What is worth getting up early for? What is worth working at for no gain, other than the joy it gives you? Is it owning a business, playing piano, speaking a foreign language, running a charity, learning to scuba-dive, journeying through the Himalayas, or writing a book? What?

But how do you handle your family and other obligations? The Triangle will teach you how to recruit others to support your vision, and you will learn to allow miracles to occur that will handle your obligations and still support your soul's mission. Just identify the vision clearly and let it be the boss; then let the Triangle work for you.

The Vision as *boss*, is the one unchangeable factor that keeps us on track, threading through everything else in our world: loss, victory, illness, and aging. It never stops calling to us, and is always leading us forward. The truth is everyone is following a vision. It may not be one he deliberately chose, it may have arisen our of insecurities or fears. And our inherent creative power is constantly empowering that vision. The question is: does that vision fulfill your soul? If you want to see what vision is guiding your life, you need only look at the results in a few areas such as, Relationships, Health, Wealth, Career, Creative Accomplishments, Contributions to Others, Spirituality and Sexual Fulfillment. If what you are experiencing in any of these areas is not what you want, then it may be that the vision that is leading you is not truly yours; if so you have fallen from grace and are inside the Triangle.

Let us take just a moment to see the difference between visions and goals because it is important to know there is a difference. The goals I suggest we write down and follow will be steps that lead us to our visions. In themselves, they are not visions because they are not callings of the soul; they are often just jobs that need to be done. Unlike a vision which is constant and unchanging until it is attained, goals may change as better paths to our visions appear. If a goal is truly on the way to a vision, the Universe will support you in accomplishing that goal. If a goal seems too difficult it may well be that there is no Universal support for it, which means it is not in alignment with the soul's plan. Forgive me for repeating several times that *the vision is boss*; a truth that is vital whether we are organizing individual lives or a massive corporate team. Our vision is where our focus and our commitment must always be. If the goal is necessary to the attainment of that vision, it will be supported and will be accomplished because we will be flowing with grace; the power of the Universe. Along this path our lives will change in ways we never dreamed—they will take on new meanings and become richer, our senses will become sharper and our days more filled with delight.

Someone in the civil rights movement of the sixties coined the phrase "Keep your eyes on the prize!" It is an excellent reminder of how to keep our vision always before us, as close as the cherry pie, so clear we can almost see, smell, touch, and taste it. A vision as clear as that pulls us to it like a magnet.

The Difference Between Vision and Fantasy

Sometimes we think we are following a vision, when in fact it is only fantasy. The fantasy field is immense and has no boundaries; we can fantasize anything, but not be empowered to create it. Fantasy is a valuable resource for creativity; when we fantasize we open our minds to endless possibilities, seeing things we think are beyond us and realizing maybe they can be true. Somewhere in that imaginary field, we may discover a vision. In these day-dreams, artists may discover something they are passionate to create; which then becomes a vision and unfolds a mission-path to its fulfillment. If the dreamer commits to that mission, he or she becomes empowered and the game is on! How to discern the difference between vision and fantasy? A fantasy is short-lived and without power; unlike a vision, it has no path of magnetic pull. When trying to capture fantasies, we are like cats chasing butterflies, constantly bouncing from one fantasy to the other and never catching any.

Do you know now what your next vision is? Perhaps you have not listened to your soul for so long that you no longer can hear it calling. When you were a child your soul spoke to you constantly about what you could be, do and have. But too many people may have told you to stop dreaming and accept your lot as a mule in harness. Here, in two steps, is a suggestion of how to reopen that door to your soul.

1. Find a time and place every day to spend at least fifteen minutes just loving yourself, have a cup of coffee or tea near a window, walk in a lovely place or take a nap, and be constantly aware that you are flowing with Universal grace.

2. Every morning for the next thirty days, the moment you wake, write in a special tablet, one thing you feel you must *be, do*, or *have* before you die. Do this again every morning without looking at what you wrote the day before, don't try to replicate or vary from what you wrote yesterday, just write what's in your heart. Don't let anyone else see what you are writing because that may limit what you write. And please, do not be confined by what you think is possible. In this exercise let your fantasies play freely. If it feels exciting, you must write it. Do this for thirty days. On the thirtieth day, look at all your entries and search for a pattern, a vision you must fulfill. It may be the thing you wrote most often, or it may be a vision that only became clear in a few entries. You'll know it because you'll think, "Wow! That would be so fantastic! Oh, if I only could!" Read on, I'll show you how you can.

Areas in which to look for visions are:

Relationships	Wealth
Career	Spirituality
Health	Creativity
Service	Adventure

You notice how, when using a TV remote control, someone steps between the remote and the set, and the remote no longer works? Well, that's the way it is with a vision; as long as I keep a clear view between me and my vision, the magnetic attraction is active and miracles are on their way. But when I let anything come between me and my vision, that line of attraction is interrupted. So I must keep my mind clear of sabotaging thoughts. Like a windshield, my wipers must be constantly erasing the storm of habitual thoughts as they bombard my mind. A good wiper is the repetition of, "Yes I can! Yes I am!" Do this as often and as many times as it takes. After a while the vision becomes more and more real and more exciting and it is easier and to keep destructive thoughts at bay. If at first it seems too much, be deliberate and stay determined.

The Mission

Our second step into Discovery is: *What is My Mission?* The Mission is the path to the Vision; it is the line of magnetic attraction that will lead me to my soul's satisfaction. My mission will challenge, reward, strengthen, and deepen me as I walk it; much the way going through an obstacle course can help make a soldier stronger. My mission will help me grow in strength and grace and will continually expand my clarity, courage and confidence. My mission will mold me, transform me, lift me up, and make me one with my Vision.

Vision = the irresistible objective
Mission = the magnetic path to the Vision

I will plan my mission step by step, always inspired toward my vision, always remembering that the vision is boss. Though my mission will be a carefully planned journey, much of it will seem magical because of the Universal power radiating between my vision and me creating things that will seem like miracles, things I could never have foreseen. Every obstacle I overcome will then strengthen me.

Here is an example from my own life of how a vision and mission can work together to create magic. After teaching the tools of this book in countries throughout Asia, I had not yet taught in China, which I considered a closed, communist country that might reject my kind of individualism. Then, one morning, when I arose from my sleep in Tokyo, I just knew I had to go teach in China. I had not planned it and it made no practical sense. It was just an idea that had slipped into my consciousness as I slept and I couldn't shake it. A vision had formed of me standing in a large auditorium talking to hundreds of people. Yet going to China seemed virtually impossible; I had no visa, nor any connections there; I knew not one person in China. Even if I were to be allowed in the country I would have no way of gathering students. But by that afternoon I could no longer ignore the vision of the large hall filled with Chinese students. I realized my soul was calling me to action, and I couldn't ignore it. Yet it was hard not to question how this improbable vision could possibly come to be.

I went to the Chinese consulate in Tokyo and was surprised when they quickly gave me a visa. Without delay I booked a flight to Beijing, still having no idea what I would do once I got there. Not since my days of free-diving alone in areas inhabited by great white sharks had I felt so insecure. Without the slightest glimmering of how I could get students or, if I could, whether the Chinese government would then arrest me for teaching my philosophies of individual empowerment, I went forward. Throughout that long day I kept converting my fear into positive energy and focused on my vision of showing the Triangle on a big board to an auditorium filled with fascinated Chinese people.

When the plane landed I realized I had no idea what the next step was. I didn't know what to do. I sat in my seat watching other passenger's stream off past me. Finally I said to myself; "Okay Bob, all you need do is take one step at a time. Get up and get your bag from the overhead. Got it? Good. Now walk off the plane, come on, one step at a time. Don't think about what you have to do after that, just do this." Step by step, following my vision, I got off the plane and went through customs which was surprisingly easy. It was all so easy!

Then I found myself standing in the lobby of the airport without the slightest idea of what to do next. I was just waiting for my soul to guide me. As I stood there watching the masses of people move around me, a well-dressed gentleman approached and introduced himself in perfect English. He asked what I was doing in Beijing, and without thinking I told him I had come to present a seminar on self-empowerment. After a few more questions he asked me to dine with him. Over a delicious lunch, he told me he had a business in Beijing and invited me to speak to his staff that afternoon.

With him translating, I spoke to his staff for three hours. They were fascinated and he was very pleased. At his expense, he booked me into an expensive hotel, took me for a marvelous dinner and asked if I would accompany him the next day to present a two day seminar in Shen Yang.

Two days later I was standing at the front of a huge audience in an auditorium that I recognized as the exact one in my vision. I spoke for two days, teaching the Triangle and other techniques of self-empowerment. The people were grateful and enthusiastic. They flooded me with gifts, introduced me to their children and treated me like a long-lost relative. My soul knew what it wanted to experience and it led me to the fulfillment of that vision. At any time I could have refused to follow that mission and gone a different direction. But then, what karmic needs were fulfilled for me and thousands of others because I followed that vision? When we follow the callings of our souls, we invariably contribute to ourselves and our global family. The toughest part for any of us is going forward with faith in a vision when we have no idea how it is going to work out. The more we practice following our visions and taking the necessary risks, the easier it is to find that faith.

There are many stories of people using these methods to accomplish things as unlikely as healing deadly diseases, to becoming award-winning authors. None of their visions was easy to attain; each of them matured spiritually, emotionally, and psychologically in the process. Because they were being guided by their souls rather than their egos, they not only were being fulfilled, they felt and looked younger and more alive.

Designing a Mission

To be successful, a mission must have two parts: Strategies and Ethics. *Strategies* are the flexible plans we make, our step-by-step goals. *Ethics* keep our mission spiritually grounded so the power will keep flowing from the Universe to support us. *Mission strategies* include such things as how we handle financing, timing, talent, logistics, recruiting team members, dealing with personalities, weather, and whatever. As we go around the Triangle, these plans may change. We will be constantly overcoming obstacles and making strategic adjustments. Because we are each pioneers on the paths of our missions, we won't ever have all the answers and, as a result will make numerous mistakes. Yet, mistakes are vital parts of the learning process, so don't let them discourage you. Above all, don't let them chase you inside the Triangle. Remember our old friend Thomas Edison? He made thousands of mistakes before he got the light bulb to glow. If he had become discouraged and given up we would still be spending our nights huddled around candles. Edison saw his vision clearly—an illuminated light bulb. He kept changing his strategies until finally his mission path led straight to the vision. We must be willing to constantly revamp our strategies too, without becoming discouraged by what did not work.

But remember, a plan is not a vision. As we move forward, we may constantly reformat our plans, but the vision will remain constant. One of the main reasons people ultimately fail in their life's missions is that they are either not clear about or committed to the vision, or they fail to alter the mission in accomplish the vision. As we plan, we must stay flexible; letting strategies adjust as they need to.

Maintaining one's honor, or ethics, is absolutely essential to reaching one's vision. Your honor is the foundation of your strength and worthiness; it is through this foundation that you receive grace, the Universal power to accomplish your mission. You hold your honor like water in cupped hands. Relaxing your ethics is like opening your fingers; when you do so, even slightly, your honor slips away and, like the water, is very difficult to regain. Even though we may have temporary achievements that result from dishonesty, cheating, stealing, oppressing, manipulating, or harming others, we will have fallen from grace and the magic will be gone from our lives. We will be out of balance with the Universe, having tipped the scales of harmony so that we fall below where we began. Thereafter we will find life to be a very hard road to travel. You simply cannot afford to make that mistake. Your honor must be intact at all times if you are to succeed consistently at your life's work. In order to build the self-confidence and self-worth necessary for continual success, we must each stay morally clean.

Who Is On My Support Team?

Once you have a vision and are developing your mission, it is time to recruit a support team, those who will support your mission; who may have talents and connections you lack and who are able to see your mission with objectivity. A team may be one person or a group; the essential ingredient being the willingness to stand with you all the way. At times the Universe may send you an angel, as happened with the gentleman in the Beijing Airport who guided me to doing my work in China. At other times support team members may be friends or family who want to serve. By sharing your vision with them, you quickly learn whether they are on your team. If they are willing, recruit them. If not, don't allow their doubts to influence your determination.

For years I was a professional singer. My family was not supportive, they thought I should get a steady job and "make something of myself." Over the years I let their opinion of me as a failure erode my self-confidence. I allowed their rejection to destroy my career. I now see that I was staying inside my comfort zone and inside the Triangle by paying attention to them. I learned that we must be very careful to not select only those who only agree with our self-doubts. We want supporters who will help us grow, who will tell us the truth even when it is difficult to hear. We want those who will keep us focused on the vision.

I discovered that we each have two families, one is the group of people to whom we are related, the other is made up of those who understand and support our dreams. Regardless of whether they are family or even close friends, be careful of letting others dilute the power of your vision or mission by skepticism. The support team member you are looking for is one who loves you and realizes that, like a young tree with the vision of a giant, you will need support in the beginning. Unless he or she sees the potential in you, don't allow them to invade your dream. Doubters can pull you down and weaken your resolve. Your dreams are sacred; you must not allow anyone the right to destroy them.

Once you have your team, let them help you strategize the steps of your mission, reminding you who you are, nudging you back on course when you begin to stray and holding your vision for you when you become discouraged. Remember, you don't need a boss here, the vision is boss; you just need another brain, another pair of eyes and ears and hands to expand your viewpoint and to make the journey easier and more enjoyable.

Lastly, make sure your support team consists of people with whom you have a *reciprocal* support agreement. It will be your duty to help them find and begin working toward their own visions. Unless support works both ways it seldom works at all. Unless those you support allow themselves to be supported by you, you could easily find yourself feeling indebted and then being controlled or manipulated.

What Is My Next Step?

Visions are most often like watermelons, too big to be taken in one bite. Those who fail here, often do so because they reach too high, trying to accomplish their entire vision in one pass around the Triangle. Change is very threatening to our egos. We cannot abandon our egos; we must train them to serve our visions instead of protecting our pasts. To do that is like teaching a child to ride a bicycle. We use training wheels and go easy until the child becomes confident. The ego must also grow to trust that our changes will be safe ones. So, following our mission strategies, we must take small, yet challenging steps and let them build confidence and clarity within us. Ultimately they will lead us to victory.

What is a good next step for you? It will be a small one, in line with your vision. It must also be one that asks you to expand your idea of yourself, expand your self-image, because if you already saw yourself as able to own your vision, you would already have it. The undeniable truth is that nothing new will come into and stay in your life until you change how you are seeing life.

You will not be changing your identity. If you now see yourself as a mother, father, friend, singer, good worker, attractive or talented, this change will not lose those identities, you will keep them and become even more. If, however, you have ideas of yourself as a failure, weak, unintelligent, or unlovable, those identities will be challenged and step by step erased. In either case, your image of yourself will expand and as it does your entire world will expand with it. Opportunities that you never dreamed of will begin coming your way.

However, you cannot create a different result using the same attitudes that created the situation you want to change. If you are poor, you cannot become wealthy keeping the same attitudes that have kept you poor. If you have failed relationships, you cannot hope to create successful ones using the methods that have left you lonely and misunderstood. To reach your vision then, you must seek change, and the change must be in your beliefs, your methods and your attitudes. As your ego limitations ease, your stubbornness relaxes and your enemies are forgiven, your vision becomes a reality. In this process of transformation we will discover wonderful new things about our abilities and our strengths. We will find ourselves being more effective in nearly every part of our lives.

A Positive Attitude

The Universal Consciousness that answers your prayers, does not recognize a negative; so when you are saying, "I *do not* want to fail here!" the Universe hears: "I ... want to fail here!" "I *don't* want to be poor!" translates to, "I ... want to be poor!" In response, the Universe then follows our direction and brings that reality about. On a deeper level this is karma at work; through our prayers and affirmations, our Creator, guiding us along a path of eternal growth, understands that we have not yet grown beyond our negatives, and sees that we stay with them until we do. We create our realities by where we focus our attention. If our mission path is focused on *running from what we detest*, rather than *creating what we love*, then what we will get is more running from what we detest. Focusing on what you do want instead of what you do not want, is something we must practice every day as we are inundated by the negatives around us; what is wrong with our finances, our relationships and our world. When surrounded by those attitudes it is too easy to focus from that viewpoint. If we will train ourselves to envision the way we want things to be and then live as though that vision is becoming a reality, miracles will begin to happen.

You may have a vision and find people telling you that you are naive, that you should face facts. But facts are always what has been, never what will be or what can be. In holding your vision you are envisioning beyond the present, into what things can be. People may argue because it is unsettling for them to see you abandon their view-point. You will need to ignore the reasons and statistics they quote to prove you can't do it; statistics are all records of what has been, not what can be. They aren't relevant to you because you are a pio-neer; you are creating a new reality, relative to nothing that has ever happened before. If your critics refuse to see that visions work mira-cles, have them check out the story of Henri Charriere who was called Papillon—French for Butterfly.

Locked away in his cell on Devils Island, an inescapable place surrounded by hungry sharks, Charriere was told again and again that no one had ever escaped from Devil's Island, that such a feat was absolutely impossible. But, as a true visionary, Papillon did not see things as they were, but as they might be. He envisioned him-self free. He willed himself to be free. He committed himself to the vision of being free. He did not have the benefit of this book or the lessons we have learned since then. But without knowing it he was enlisting the power of the Universe by holding his vision. The mag-netic vibration within him correlated with the vibrating Universe and his vision held that vibration in place through all the doubts and problems he encountered. Henri Charriere not only escaped and became a free man, he also became very wealthy and the book, *Papillon*, became a best-seller and a movie. So no matter how diffi-cult your situation may now seem, you are not locked in a cell on an island surrounded by hungry man-eating sharks. You escape from your situation not by focusing on it, but by focusing beyond it, on what you are envisioning.

Tell those who say you are too young, too tall, too short, the wrong race, the wrong gender, or whatever, to ask Tara Lipinski. This fourteen-year-old girl challenged all veteran superstar skaters in the world and beat them when she won The World Skating Championship. Unbelievable? The next year she faced them again and they were prepared for her. But it was to no avail and Tara Lipinski became the youngest person in Olympic history to win a gold medal.

Neither Henri Charriere nor Tara Lipinski is more capable of vision-inspired heroism than you. When you are as committed to your vision as they were to theirs, you'll be just as successful, regardless of what obstacles may face you.

On my flight from Beijing to Shen Yang I was glued to the window, watching the great land of China unravel below me. I saw there, a sight that has inspired me since. I saw rivers flowing through valleys, each one heading toward the sea. From my lofty viewpoint I could see what the rivers could not, that they were destined to be interrupted constantly by towering mountains. I studied what the rivers did when they came to these obstacles. The ones that stood their ground, trying to push a mountain out of their way lost their identities as rivers; they became lakes. The rivers that were willing to constantly alter their mission plans in order to stay in motion toward their goal, which was to join with the sea, did not resist the mountains, they simply caressed their flanks as they slipped around them on and went on their way. From each mountain they gained strength and volume. Our problems, like mountains can halt our progress and keep us focused on them until finally solving those problems becomes our life's work just as dissolving mountains becomes the work of trapped rivers. But we are eternal souls, not lakes, and we are here on missions to discover and grow. We must keep moving toward our visions; we cannot let obstacles stop our forward motion. In the process of moving forward, we will discover that many of the problems that occupy our time, don't need to be resolved by us; they just need to be addressed, caressed and released.

A friend had an old car in his yard for years; he was looking for a used transmission for it. He would not sell it because he was focused on fixing it. His vision was not that of having transportation, it was of fixing that old car, in which his chickens had by now taken roost. But the transmission he wanted was hard to find. Then, after several years, his father-in-law gave him a car and he released the truck and moved on. Here again is the value of a good support team; it keeps us focused on what is truly important, encouraging us to release the old and embrace the new. In creating relationships that work, this may mean forgiving old debts and starting over clean, caressing those old mountains and moving on.

Deciding your next step will require you to focus on what you want, not what you don't want. Instead of getting rid of a disease, focus on the part of you that is healthy. Instead of the job you don't like, focus on what you do want in your career. For example: focus on being wealthy instead of thinking how to get out of poverty. Whatever you decide is your next step, make it small; remember a watermelon can only be eaten one bite at a time. Most people who fail at their missions do so because they try to do too much at one time. Love and pace yourself and make this journey as fun and easy as possible.

Where are we now on the Triangle? We have discovered our vision, laid out our mission, recruited a support team and now are ready to start creating. If this is my path, I am realizing at this point, that in order for me to bring about a new reality, I must change myself, my attitude and my beliefs. The experiences of thousands of people around the world have taught us that nothing in our lives can change until we make space for it by changing *how* we think.

Choose either Risk or Anxiety

The entire outside of the Triangle is energized. One name for that energy field is excitement, another is fear. There is always fear—pure energy. If we use that energy in a positive way we will do what we never dreamed we could. But this energy is alive and moving; if we do not harness and direct it, it will harness and direct us to inside the Triangle. If we resist change because we are afraid, that energy will force us into Anxiety and then paralyze us. The energy of fear is constant; we must choose how to use it. Risk is fear actualized. Anxiety is fear resisted.

Changing, for us humans, is the scariest thing. It is also an opportunity to see if we are more than we thought we were. If our vision is truly the calling of our soul, this process will be so empowering that it will lead us to success.

Our vision is sending out lines of magnetic vibration, drawing us to it, miraculously removing the obstacles in our way, but still, our vision cannot come to us; we must *grow* to it. To accomplish this we must let go of things that pull us down; we must drop our weights, like a hot-air balloon drops its ballast to rise; discarding old beliefs and ideas that restrict our expansion. How? By remembering that *the vision is boss*. If a belief or idea hinders the vision, it must be released, changed or expanded. Those who don't drop their vision-defeating ballast will be pulled back down into Anxiety.

As you can see, the steps we took along the Discovery side of the Triangle were all questions. They set us up to then do our sacred work. The steps along the Risk and Self-Love sides are all affirmations that start with the words I am, such as: I am Changing My Identity. Being constantly aware of where you are on the Triangle and repeating the affirmations again and again will help you dissolve your confusion and self-doubts.

I Am Expanding My Identity

I cannot have a new life without changing my identity. What do I mean by identity? It is the place within me from which I relate to the world. The matrix of things that make up who I think I am are all titles such as: I am man, I am a woman, I am a child, I am smart, I am always failing, I am always winning, I am needy, I am helpless, I am not well educated, I am incompetent at certain things, I am lonely, I am wealthy, I am usually misunderstood, I am doing the best I can, I am incapable of changing my life, I am just like my mother, I am just like my father, I am a failure, I am unworthy of having all my dreams come true, etc.

I'm sure you could fill a book with your self-images. But they are mountains that restrict your passage to the sea and, if you are to fulfill yourself in this lifetime, you must expand beyond those identities to see yourself having all the power and imagination of your soul. If a teacher in the second grade said you were just not good at math, there is a good chance you might accept that opinion, make it a part of your identity and be poor at math for the rest of your life. And then, how can you ever get beyond that identity unless you are pulled out of it by a vision? Because you believed it, it became a part of your identity, your Basic Operating System. (BOS)

I Am Focused On My Vision

If we keep the vision before us, keep our eyes on the prize and let its excitement inspire us, will we be empowered to overcome whatever obstacles the Universe throws at us. Wait! Why would a beneficent Universe be throwing obstacles in our way? Because it knows that only by overcoming them will we grow in confidence, strength and grace. Along this mission path are these experiences the soul needs for its fulfillment. It is through these experiences that the soul will dance with the Universe and experience completeness and joy. You are being divinely guided as long as you keep focused on your vision. Completeness and joy can become daily experiences for you when you walk the Triangle every day.

I Am Working My Mission

At this point you know your mission: strategy with honor. Your vision and mission are clearly in mind. Now is the time to take those steps, one at a time. The taking of those steps do two things; they change us forever and they take us to our vision. These changes are sometimes painful for those who have been living in an identity of self-pity or chronic failure because they demand that we rise above those old identities and establish new ones. Following the steps we have laid out to our vision, we recognize that this discomfort is like a birth pain. If we do not give up now, we will change our entire lives and become more powerful than we ever dreamed. If we find that our plan needs to be altered, we will be flexible enough to do whatever it takes, within the scope of our ethics and honor, to make the path to our vision easier.

Sometimes when I find myself feeling unsettled, I realize I'm on the Risk side of the Triangle and I have not planned my mission as well as I should. I am staggering around, banging into walls instead of making progress. I may have committed to my vision without committing to the necessary changes within myself. This pain I go through has a purpose; it is telling me something is not right, in this case, that I'm off my path, that I need to wake up and get my mission straight. I realize I need to turn my mental lights on and start looking at where I'm going. I need courage now.

Though my dictionary defines courage as having the ability to face danger without fear, I see courage as being willing to harness fear's energy to my mission. Big risks take big courage which is why fear is then stronger—to give us more energy. But real courage requires trust, or as the ancients called it; *faith.* To build faith we need constant wins so we know we are blessed; that we have the ability to always overcome our difficulties. One reason the Triangle is so valuable is that it trains us to take only the size of risks for which we have either trust or courage, and to then increase the sizes of risks as our confidence grows. Imagine how your confidence, courage and clarity will have grown when you have used the Triangle diligently for one year. Long before then, the steps will have become second nature to you.

Why is Risk so difficult? So scary? Because we are being transformed; parts of our egos are dying and are being reborn and the ego does not die quietly. The good news is that as it dies it is reborn with a new identity, one that gives us a fuller and richer life. That reward is just around the corner; so don't give up! If you feel overly distressed by the Risk part of the Triangle, try repeating: "I'm changing now and though it feels distressing, it is not dangerous." Just keep your eyes on the prize and soon you will have won.

I Am Contributing

In this last step on the Risk side, you can see that you are making a contribution to your community and to the Universe. By fulfilling your mission, you are building your boat—doing your part in the Universe. By reaching for your vision, you inspire and empower others around you. Because you are unique among all creatures that have ever lived, your transformation, brings into the Universe a new dimension, one that can only come from you. Children are watching you, adults talk about you, admiring your courage, praying for your success and modeling themselves after you. Step one in helping people you love move out from inside the Triangle is to stay on the outside yourself. By your example you are leading the way, opening a window of light into a world that for some seems totally sealed off.

The *Win* corner of the Triangle is the winner's circle, the medal-awarding area! Because it is so often overlooked, this may be the most important of all corners of the Triangle for us to focus on. It is in Win that we begin to truly change the way we see ourselves and our place in the world. It is here that we begin to build the confidence necessary to live full, happy and productive lives. But this is also the place where we easily slip into old patterns of unworthiness and thereby lose all we have gained. In order to stay on the outside of the Triangle here, you must acknowledge that you have won, that you have challenged your fears and insecurities and taken a step away from then towards freedom.. You are a winner because you took appropriate risks and rose above your self-doubts. You now have the right and even a duty to yourself to be in joy, grateful for being who you are.

I know that your vision may not have yet been fully accomplished, it may take more turns around the Triangle to attain that, but you are on your way, and growing with every step. Remember, it is easy to fall into unworthiness and thereby lose the confidence and excitement you have earned. This is due to the fact that many of us have been taught that it is virtuous to downplay our successes. We think it is humble to tell ourselves we should have done better. But real humility is not based on falseness; it is anchored in truth. The Triangle is a tool for breaking old habitual ways of thinking and establishing healthy new ones. Though it is always challenging, it is life-changing for those who do not give up.

Perhaps you thought if you went around the Triangle once you should feel totally free and joyous. It doesn't quite work that way, the Triangle path must become a daily routine and then you will see a new you awakening. The process of building joy may be gradual, but every single day of your life will be more joyous than the one before if you just follow these steps. How can it be better than that? Just make a decision to win the day—every day.

Winning the Day

What does it take for you to win the day? Set your vision and accomplish at least one step toward its fulfillment today and you will have won the day! Only one good win at any time during the day wins the entire day for you. If you win four days this week, you will have won the week! If you win three weeks this month you will have won the month! Think of how your life will change in one year; having acknowledged 260 winning days, imagine the self-confidence, courage and commitment to life you will have built! But in order for those wins to do their job of building your confidence, they must be acknowledged. So today I must say "I have won this day!" And then, "I have won this week!" And "I have won this month!" Just imagine what it will be like to live in that atmosphere of winning all the time. All it will require is your commitment to let your vision lead you around and around the Triangle.

Choose Either Self-Love or Unworthiness

So at Win, we choose either self-love or self-loathing, it is that clear! You may say to yourself, "I could have done it better; I should have done it better." If so you may not go into Self-Love, you must allow the darkness to pull you down into Unworthiness. If, on the other hand, you say, "I'm out here doing my best and I'm growing every day," then you may go into Self-Love and begin healing and truly romancing your soul. Please take the time to read these affirmations carefully and see if they are at all difficult for you. If so, then there may be some old self-deprecating beliefs that need healing. As you read the words of these affirmations, please realize that without the commitment to actually change our attitudes, the words mean very little. We must do more than just say the words, we must live them. For example; how does a person who feels *loved* behave? How does a person who feels *blessed* behave? How does a person who feels *safe* behave? How does a person who feels *free* behave? I awaken in the night, troubled by a thought or a dream and say these affirmations dozens of times. Or I may select only one or two such as: "I am blessed, I am safe." While doing so, I fall asleep and my subconscious continues building a platform of confidence and security within me. Whenever you are feeling doubtful about yourself, these affirmations can lead you to thinking right, thinking truth and will eventually become the foundation blocks of your new identity. Let's look at each of them individually:

I Am Loved

Love is natural; it is grace, the flowing creative power of the Universe. Are you loveable? Of course you are. But if you feel you are not, that attitude will push away all who want to love you. If you feel you are not loveable, it is because you are inside the Triangle and not seeing truth clearly. If you were not loved, you could not be alive right now, reading this. But it may be new to actually admit you are loved, and to recognize how many people love you. It is accepting grace in its purest form to realize this. You are loved and you are loving others, loving life, loving being alive, loving helping and seeing others win at their own Triangles of life. You are in the flow of grace and are being healed and empowered. Now, to know and live it as truth; that is our goal.

If the process of training yourself to feel all the love, the grace that is available ford you seems hard; don't give up! Learning to think in a different way, means seeing yourself from a new viewpoint. As you experience this affirmation you will begin to know yourself more and more as loveable, loved and loving. You couldn't possibly be any deeper in self-loathing and self-pity than I was before I started following the Triangle out of that maze. I was a victim, convinced I had a tough life with none of the opportunities afforded to others. I thought my never-winning identity was permanent, but affirmations set me free. They worked because I was following a vision of myself as I am now. Thousands of us have healed our souls by letting our Visions carry us around the Triangle, teaching us who we really are. So if feeling loved is difficult for you; try saying (and meaning) *I am loveable and I am loved* fifty times, four times a day for ten days. Then see how different life seems. And meanwhile, behave as though it is true and watch as miracles begin to happen.

I Am Blessed

How could you be anything other than blessed? Has there ever been, or will there ever be another you; another person with your delicate fingerprints, with your eyes, your brain structure, voice, and viewpoint? You are blessed because you are singular and unique; you see and think and do as no other person ever has. Your life is being guided by Holy Spirit, the Creative Force that brought you here and led you to be thinking the thoughts this book is awakening within you. You are an eternal soul on a temporary physical journey to expand in joy and wisdom. You have talents and opportunities ready to unfold if you will accept them. Greater treasures than you have ever imagined are yours, waiting now for you to claim them.

I Am Safe

Look back now, over your life and recognize some of the many times you could have been severely injured or even killed and yet were safe; of the times you have been exposed to deadly diseases, or didn't know how you would possibly get through the day, or the night and yet you were always safe. How could this happen unless you are being protected? Even though you have sometimes taken gambles that could have destroyed you, some force was always there, carefully guiding you to safety. When you finally give up doubting, you can do more than you ever dreamed of. While it is true that one day we will each leave this dimension, even then, in the act of dying, we will be safe, pure souls, filled with grace and protected by the love of Great Spirit. But you can't know this if you don't pay attention to your life, to how often you are guided to the right place at the right time. You are safe; please know that!

Rest

Now you must stop and realize who you are, who you must be, in order to have made the Triangle journey you just completed. When challenged by fear, you found the courage to convert it into pure energy. You defined a vision, designed a mission, committed to it and completed the first step. You took the risks necessary to challenge and expand the limits of your old identity. It may have been difficult at times but you did not give up. You won and acknowledged your accomplishment and your growth by accepting the win and loving yourself without shame. You made the first step on your mission path and if you continue, you will certainly have your vision. You have proven that you are not your past, you are not your experiences, and that there is nothing you cannot change.

Now, having made that assessment of yourself, let your mission and vision fade into the background. Change your focus from *doing* and having, to just *being*. This is a time of Rest, of restoration. Thinking about where you will go from here will be counterproductive to your ultimate goal and will take you out of Rest before you're ready. This is a time to simply nurture yourself. It is a time to feel grateful.

Gratitude is the platform of your personal power. While writing this book, and realizing that every has value to you, none is more important than gratitude because it is the platform of creative power. It is so important that I found it difficult to know where to put it so that you, the reader, would see its value. Gratitude, simply stated, is the foundation without which no creative effort can become successful. Without gratitude we have no base for creating anything new. It is as simple as that. With gratitude our souls open to an unlimited flow of grace. How do we find what to be grateful for? First, we take careful inventory of our lives today, as we are right now, and see what blessings we can find. If we are careful in our search, we will be amazed. There were dark times in my life when I would have said, "I don't see any blessings." I had been concentrating on my pain and loss so much I had forgotten there was anything else. Now I know that the surest way to heal and revitalize myself is to take stock of *all* the good things in my life.

Gratitude is like looking in your bank-book and discovering you are wealthier than you thought. Here is a simple exercise: take a blank sheet of paper, divide it with a line down its center. Head one column with the word *Blessing*s and the other with the word *Curses*. Now start in either place and make as many entries as you can. If you are finding it hard to write your blessings, think of what you cannot be without: your body, your mind, thoughts, dreams, plans, friends, love, food, water, air, life, a roof over your head, a bed, TV, radio, books, etc. These are simple ones, you will discover many more in your life including all your experiences, both joyful and painful, that have taught you and made you strong and wise. We are daily given blessings we often don't see.

I was coming out of my mailbox facility last week and saw a sunset I will never forget. Of all the sunsets I have seen at sea, in the dessert and in the mountains, this was one of the top ten. I hurried back into the shop and told the clerks about it: "You must come outside and see this sunset; it is really amazing." Only one lady walked to the door and looked out for a moment. "It's nice." she said. "My husband is an artist. I know he'd like to see that" Then she was gone. I looked around the busy parking lot, people coming and going from stores and cars, not one of them saw the splendor dancing over their heads. As I watched the colors change from bright reds and yellows to maroon and finally purple, I noticed the first evening star. I asked myself again: what is the reason for a sunset or sunrise to be so colorful? How does it sci-entifically benefit nature? There can only be one answer: this is a gift from God, a free, daily gift to remind us how loved all of us are. But most of us are too busy with our important thoughts to receive these treasures. The more we practice gratitude, the more of these blessings we'll become aware of. Joy is the food of the soul and gratitude is one of the greatest joymakers. As you become aware of your blessings, they each awaken the romance in your soul. When we are grateful, we are romanced by new things every day; like clouds and laughter and our skins.

Simply by being grateful then, you become more effective in everything you do, have more peace of mind and a better understanding of yourself as a very special and privileged being. So begin by finding whatever you can find to be grateful for, concentrate on that and let it grow until you feel yourself being totally blessed. Then self-confidence builds and you will relax in the knowledge that you always have and always will win at life.

When I see a Christmas tree I imagine each ornament as one of my blessings and realize anew that every one of my life experiences is as bright and shining in my soul as are those ornaments on the tree. But no tree could possibly hold all the beautiful experiences of my life including those that were sweet and fed my soul, and those that were bitter that made me stronger and wiser. At the Rest corner of the Triangle I am restored by this awareness that becomes the joy and confidence that empowers my next venture.

Habits Become Addictions

As we pass around the Triangle we are overcoming habits that have limited us. It is not easy, we must fight for what we want, and usually the fight is against our old, anchored lifestyles. You can now see the difference in actively choosing, as opposed to letting your life be controlled by habit. The ego loves habit, loves sameness even when that sameness is destructive; the ego resists change by applying on us such techniques such as terror, anxiety, confusion and procrastination. We cannot afford ego to run our lives. We must keep growing because otherwise we are declining, dying. Growth is not possible without change and dreams cannot come true unless we change our attitudes and our feelings about ourselves.

To give you an example of how insidious habit is; there was a dirt road on a ranch where I lived as a boy. In the wintertime, the road into the pasture became so deeply rutted by tractor tires going around the corner from the lane that by early summer we wouldn't even have to steer the tractor because the wheels would just follow the rutted tracks all by themselves. Like that tractor going into the pasture, we have cut ruts into our consciousness so that we make the same choices over and over again without even thinking about it. Unlike rutted roads, we can change our minds and in doing it, change our lives. Every time we consciously go around the Triangle, deliberately staying on the outside, we are erasing old rut-habits and expanding our futures. Our courage also expands as does our self-confidence and our lives widen and deepen. We are enriched and empowered every time we go around the outside of the Triangle.

Habits eventually become addictions. We must be honest about what the benefits are from addictive behavior. For example; feeling like a failure, means we don't have to accomplish anything in order to validate ourselves. Self-pity is like a warm blanket in which we can hide. Resentment toward others frees us from accepting that we, not they, are controlling our lives. Each time we go around the Triangle we take a bite out of those addictions and form new identities as winners and creators. We may fall back a few times before we find ourselves free of that pattern, free of going inside the Triangle; but if we keep making the vision the boss in all things, eventually those old patterns will be replaced by those that empower us.

The moment you realize you are inside the Triangle, the first step is to figure out how you got there. At which corner did your self-sabotage happen? *Discovery vs. Avoidance? Risk vs. Anxiety?* Or *Self-Love vs. Unworthiness?* Then you can go back to that place and remake that choice and go outside the Triangle. It's important to come out at the same place you went in because that is where your work needs to be done on an old habit. That is the place where you must practice making the right decision. Nothing on your mission path will function like it should until that bit of business is handled.

Here is a simple example: You are applying for a new job. At the Change corner, you slip into Anxiety instead of taking the Risk to put yourself forward with all your lights turned on. You let your fears intimidate rather than energize you and you sank into Paralysis. But wait! You recognize what is happening, and then go back and choose to take the Risk. "Excuse me sir; in my meeting with you, I became too anxious and didn't give you the best of me. I'd like another chance to show you who I am and what I can do for your company." If the answer is no, or if you don't get the job for any reason, you still have converted your fear to excitement and blown apart the old identity that was sabotaging you. You will find it much easier to apply for the next job or the next, always staying on the outside as you move through the process. The goal is to be in charge of our lives by always making the right choices.

I was inside the Triangle for years. It seemed a safe place for me because it validated who I thought I was. I didn't risk so I didn't have to worry about failing, which I appreciated at the time because I thought failure was fatal. I didn't understand that by not taking risks I was failing all the time; failing to be, to do and to have what was meant for me in this life. I actually felt a comfort in my self-pity and remorse. I was part of a community of wounded souls who all sympa-

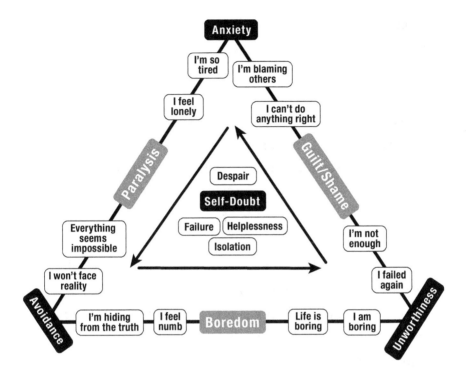

thized with each others weaknesses. We loved telling each other how awful our lives were and gossiping about villains we saw victimizing us. It was our way of feeling important, of celebrating how tough our lives were. Our soap opera would be called *Life Inside the Triangle*. One script might go something like this:

"Hello, Janice, is that you, honey?"

"Yeah!" Sniffle.

"What's wrong? Why . . . Janice, are you crying?"

Sniffle. "Oh, it's nothing."

"Oh, come on now; what's happened?"

Sigh, tremulous voice. "Oh it's just Al again."

"Damn him! What, what did he do this time?"

"Oh, Sarah, I don't want to talk about it, OK?"

"Sure, honey, sure, whatever you say."

"I mean, he hits me and he treats me like dirt." Crying now, "Oh, what good is talking about it going to do?"

"You're right, honey. It's just that I feel so bad for you. I could just kick that butthead."

"Well," Janice bites back her sobs. "It's no worse than your son being in jail for drugs, is it? I mean, he was just in the wrong place at the wrong time. Neither of us have a very easy road here. And there's not a damn thing we can do about it."

"No, honey; we sure didn't get any breaks in this life, that's for sure."

"All I said to him is . . . and this was last night . . . I said: 'Al, I don't think you should have another drink.' And then he went into this rage and started breaking a chair against the wall. I tried to stop him. I guess I shouldn't have. I know what always happens."

"Then he hit you?"

"With the chair, I think he broke my ribs."

"Honey, you need to go to the hospital!"

"No, no, I'll be all right. I've had them broken before. You just have to go through a lot of pain for a couple of weeks."

"But maybe the doctor could wrap you up or something?"

"We don't have the money for a doctor; you know that, Sarah."

"Oh, damn. I just wish I could help you. I just wish I had some money, but you know Clyde's laid off now, and we're just barely getting by."

Any of this sound familiar? When we tune in tomorrow, we'll find that Janice started coughing up blood, but still refused to go to the doctor. Sarah will be so distraught over Janice's condition; she will have a couple of drinks, which means she is off the wagon again. Then, because of it, she will fall into a deep depression; with her husband out of work and her son in jail; she will decide to kill herself. That cliffhanger ends, but in the next episode, Sarah will be saved from doing herself in by learning that Janice was just found unconscious on her kitchen floor and rushed to the hospital. Then on Friday's episode we will find Sarah and wife-beater, Al waiting together outside the emergency-room door. In a fit of remorse, Al will break down and tell Sarah how he lost control and hit Janice only when he discovered she was having an affair with, guess who? Sarah's husband, Clyde! Now all our characters are fully enmeshed in the paralysis, guilt, and shame. We can't be sure they're in Boredom yet, but we certainly know we are. What a mess!

It is true, of course, that when we live outside the Triangle, we lose this kind of drama and we may lose our pity-partners as well. But that drama is addicting; I know that because it was an addiction I grew up with, not one that I loved, but one that formed my comfort zone. I didn't know there was another option. I recognized that there were people winning at life and moving upward but I knew I was not like them; they were as different from my family and me, as if they had come from another planet. They were born with privileges I was neither allowed to have nor understand. Because of who they were, they would always get breaks that were unavailable to me. This is the attitude of a classic underdog, mentality eroding its soul with self-fulfilling prophesies.

No matter how many thousands of flight hours a pilot might have, when getting ready to take off, he or she first goes over the checklist. The Triangle is your checklist and your map to success. Use the Triangle as a navigation plan and you'll learn to never crash again! You'll fly higher in life, constantly gaining confidence and personal power, and your fear of fear will never again trap you. After only one week of using the Triangle, most people are more creative and more relaxed, feel better and look better. After a few weeks they notice their relationships, their health and their wealth significantly improved and every part of their lives functioning at its best. After one year, people are living the lives they dreamed of. Whatever you imagine you can be, do or have, it is yours if you will simply follow the path outside the Triangle. Leon would suggest that you don't wait, that you start building your boat right now!

CHAPTER FOUR

THE ANCIENT SECRET TO WEALTH IS JOY

◇◇◇◇◇◇◇

A Matter of Choice

We often believe that our decisions are dictated by our circumstances, but that idea makes circumstances our masters instead of our creations. In this chapter you will find the secret behind every truly successful person who has ever lived on this planet. It is a secret that has several parts, like a cake recipe. Understanding and accepting the facts that make up this truth has changed the lives of thousands of my students; made them wealthy, helped them put diseases into remission, led them to their soul-mates, empowered them to overcome disabilities and taught all of them to love being alive. A most interesting thing about the secret is this: everyone knows it. It is like a chunk of solid gold laying next to everyone's doorstep, being stepped over every day by people who think it is just a rock in the yard.

During the past thirty years as a personal coach and trainer, I studied the attitudes of people who were struggling and the attitudes of those I considered successful. The successful ones were those who created their own realities, who bounced back from disappointment and lived with laughter in their hearts. Some were wealthy, some were famous, others successful in individual ways. The one factor they all have in common is this: they realize that *everything they experience is the result of their own choices.* (Part one of the secret!) When they look back over their lives, they don't blame others for their sorrows, heartbreaks, failures, or losses; nor do they credit others for their joys, loves, successes, or achievements. They acknowledge that their lives are guided in every way by the choices they make. *This personal accountability, more than any other single factor, determines who will be losers or winners, poor or wealthy, lonely or loved, trapped or free.* It determines who will be on the outside of the Triangle and who will be on the inside. Again, these winners accept that everything they experience is the result of their choices.

Can you think of situations that don't appear to be the result of choices? Here is a question a young man in one of my classes asked:

"My uncle died in a plane crash. Are you telling me that was his choice?"

"My answer is no, of course not! I am saying his death in the plane crash was a result of his choice to fly on that plane, at that time."

"But, he didn't have a choice, it was his job."

"I'm not saying he was wrong. I'm saying he chose to get on that plane. His boss didn't tie him up and force him aboard. And incidentally; didn't he choose that job?"

"Yes, but . . . are you saying he should have known the plane was going to crash?"

"No, not at all."

"Then how can you blame him for being on it when it crashed?"

"There is no *blame*; nor am I judging his decisions, I am only saying he chose to be on the plane. Giving his employer the right to make the choice for him was also his choice."

"But if you acknowledge he couldn't have known the plane was going to crash, then what's your point? How could he make a different choice if he couldn't see the future?"

"His experience of falling out of the sky was the direct result of his choice to go up into the sky. It's that simple."

If we learn to follow our true visions, the calling of our souls, we are most often protected from danger. Because we cannot predict the future, we may still occasionally make choices that result in heart-wrenching experiences to which we are guided because our souls need to grow through them.

I have been through several life experiences that were as bad as any hell could be; some of which went on for years. I felt them crushing me day and night and I thought I would die from the agony. Looking back, I now see they did the opposite of crushing me, they made me strong, they gave me viewpoints of reality I had never seen, they gave me a wisdom I could never had gained any other way. And they taught me about making good choices as surely as running my car into a tree would have taught me to pay attention to the road. Much of who I am to others in the world was formed out of those dark times. Now, if you look back on your times of suffering, hopefully you will see that they gave you strength and wisdom too. Just imagine how much less you would be now without having the blessings of those experiences.

When we accept that we are creating our own realities, every day, by the choices we make, we then understand how to recover when we are in trouble; simply begin making new choices. But if we feel we are simply the pawns of fate, then where is our hope? Our choices are these: we choose to act or to react, to take action or to refuse to take action. All are choices and all results are ours. We sometimes learn to make good choices by making bad ones. When we are children we should be allowed to make some wrong choices for that very reason so we can gain the wisdom and confidence to make good choices. Parents, who don't let their children fail, prohibit them from learning to win.

Now I'm saying our experiences are the results of our choices. Then what about children who are molested or abused? Am I saying that's their choice?

I, and many others, believe that, as eternal beings, we chose this incarnation in order to experience an aspect of existence we had not encountered before; we came to fulfill our souls, to fulfill our karma. From this point of view, a soul will set up a path before entering this world that might purposely take him or her through some abuse. In setting up this scenario, a soul knows it will survive and even grow from the experience. Yet, common sense also tells us that until children are old enough to make sensible and safe choices, we must choose for them, and we must be accountable for the results of those choices. Our choices are to act, to react or to do nothing. A parent, aware that children are being abused by the another parent, can either act by calling the authorities, react by attacking the other parent, or do nothing. Since children's experiences are often the result of choices made by the community, we are obligated to make societal choices that are good for kids.

So, what about disease? Did I choose this cold? Did my mother chose to have terminal heart disease, or my aunt her cancer?

When I caught a cold last month, it was probably because I allowed myself to get run-down. I had stopped taking my vitamin C, hadn't eaten enough vegetables and fruit in my diet for over a month, went to places where infectious germs were present; and allowed myself to become stressed. I made dozens of choices that resulted in my cold. If I had made other choices I likely would not have caught the cold. At times I have discovered that a cold or illness has kept me from attending an affair I really didn't want to attend. Would it have been more accountable to just say no? Yes, in retrospect it would have.

My mom had heart disease. It killed her at age forty-six, a tragedy I know she would have liked to avoid. But her life-choices were weak and uninformed; she was overweight, did not exercise and was highly stressed. She ate foods high in cholesterol, saturated fats and sugars. Sometimes she smoked and drank. The men she chose to father her children were lost little boys, none of whom could support her needs. She had too many children and lived in constant poverty. She could have made any number of different choices to avoid the heart attack that took her life, but she did not know that, did not have the advantage of this book's teachings. If I see my Mom as a victim, then I have to view her as powerless. I cannot do that because I grew up with that marvelous woman and I saw her power every day. She just did not know that she was a pure divine soul on a divine mission. She didn't know that she had the power to change her life.

But surely you can't prevent disease just by making a choice?

Oh sure you can; a choice can change anything! When we think forward thoughts, along the line of our visions, miracles can and do happen. After all, the future is not written, so how will it come about? Who will design it? Will it just be by chance, or by the collective thoughts of creators? Your future and your health and wealth are in your hands; or should I say, in your mind? Physicists have proven that thoughts are real things that go out into our world and create realities including the physical nature of our bodies and our surroundings.

But sometimes we would rather just let the river take us where it wants. But the river is ours and it is going where we direct it. True, it is sometimes wise to let things go and at other times, wisest to control things. But we keep the vision before us as our leader; we will know which choice will result in the rewards we want. Consider the story of the man who took his car to the top of the steepest street in town, released the brake (birth), and let it begin to roll down the hill (life), then got in the backseat and covered his head. There he stayed as the car picked up speed, damaging and destroying cars, pets, and people; knocking off two fire hydrants and flattening a flower shop. When the demolished car finally banged to a stop against the seawall at the bottom of the hill, the police were right there to arrest the driver and take him off to jail. But all the while he was protesting; "Hey, I was in the back seat, I was just a passenger."

The question is, whose car is it? Whose life is it? Not making a choice is still a choice, isn't it? And the results will be our responsibility, not someone else's. We can't opt out of our roles as creators by simply refusing to make choices. Just as today is the result of yesterday's choices, tomorrow will be the result of the choices we make today. If we let our visions be our bosses, and make our choices along that path, they will always be the right ones.

Question: What choice does a person have whose life has been predetermined? Say by illness, birth defects, or genetics?

Well, does any event keep us from making choices? Laura is riding in an airplane; gets up to go to the back for a cup of tea, leans against the door, and falls out. Laura is shocked and astonished! She can't believe it! But there she is, with the airplane's sound fading as it swims away across the sky leaving her tumbling through the cold, clear air. Laura is falling to her death, now that seems to be for sure. Like someone with a terminal illness or a genetic defect, her path seems to be laid and unchangeable. Below her, she sees farms, tiny squares on the face of the earth. They are rapidly becoming larger. She even sees birds flying beneath her.

Question: Okay so she chose to take the plane, and she chose to get a cup of tea, and she chose to lean against the door. But now her choices are used up, her life is over, right?

No, it's not over at all. Not any more than it's over for the people with birth defects or the terminal illnesses that were mentioned. She still has life, and where there is life, there are choices.

Question: What choices?

She can scream and flail. She can roll up in a ball and groan. She can open her arms and try to fly, or she can flip over on her back and look at the sky. She can sing a song, recite a poem, or say a prayer. She can study the farms below to see how many are lush and green and how many are barely making it. She has lots of choices. She can even choose not to choose. I acknowledge that will be hard to do with death rushing at her, but then, that's her present situation; sometimes we have to grow where we're planted.

Question: Get real! Laura is going to grow? Now? While she knows she's going to die? So now she's going to sing or watch farms or try to fly? C'mon, how long can she do that? Think a moment before you answer. . . . How long can Laura experience joy?

The answer. . . . For the rest of her life!

Just like you and me; whether we have fifty seconds or fifty years, it is our lifetime and our choice of how to live it. Why not chose joy?

What choices shall we make for the rest of our lives?

The Incredible Power of Joy

Joy is the state of a person outside the Triangle, even when the struggles are challenging, because true joy is neither dependent upon happiness nor diminished by sorrow. It is the spiritual foundation that keeps life in perspective through all its storms. It is our spiritual-emotional-physical balance; the food of the soul. Joy is the state we must be in before we can bring our visions to us; it is the receptor for the Creator's homing beacon and it cannot find us unless we are radiating joy. *Your joy does not come from making dreams come true. Dreams can only come true when you are in joy!* (Part two of the secret!)

Joy is the natural state of a healthy human being and is the food of the soul. We see joy in young children and watch it fade as they grow older. Why does it fade? Is its loss a part of growing up? Is it the result of losing confidence in our ability to make things work out? Does our insecurity cripple our capacity for joy? When we are not in joy, our souls begin to starve and lose communication with our minds. As the body is the constant creation of the soul, we may soon become physically diseased (dis-eased). Over the years, working with thousands of students in many countries, it has been constantly proven to me that joy is indispensable to making visions come true. Students may assimilate intellectual material from my trainings and be able to repeat it on a test, but they will not be able to apply it to their lives unless it is integrated with joy. We may be able to understand intellectually, but if we are not joyful, the windows to our souls close and nothing gets in or out.

Pierre Teilhard de Chardin taught us that joy is the *only* evidence of God. I think he would also agree that joy is the very presence of God. To choose joy is to become one with God. To commit oneself to living according to one's divine mission and stay on that course is to choose a life of joy. There is no greater gift we can give ourselves or those around us, than to be joyful; it is the purest act of Self-Love and it becomes the pathway to loving others.

For many, many years, an accepted method of getting errant children back on track has been to whack them or to dilute their self-respect with criticism. Our youngsters are watching us and learning how to discipline their future kids, just as we watched adults when we were their age. They are our students and our examples are classes they never skip. By our examples, (not by our words) they learn to either become winners or victims. If we believe we are not worthy of joy, then they will believe the same of themselves. Then, like ice cream bars left on a hot sidewalk, their sweet young souls will melt away without even being tasted.

As children we feel secure when adults protect us. But what adults must be protecting is a child's ability to feel and express joy; the joy that will sustain him when our support is no longer available. When raised without joy, we become adults who live in survival rather than self-expression. When we are not in joy we must use *force* to accomplish what we want; force exhausts us and makes us old. When in joy and following our missions, we don't need force because the natural *power* of the universe is flowing through us. We stay young and light.

Then we can make the necessary changes in our lives with joy and not be pulled into anxiety, which surely is an absence of joy. Joy is the place of quiet power within that balances the grief of loss. Joy is the foundation of creative passion. Because we are so often inundated with problems and problem people, staying in joy can feel like a tightrope on which we are trying to stay balanced. The natural state of children is to be laughing all the time, quickly forgiving each other and refusing to worry. Isn't it written that a child shall lead the way? Well, then let's allow the child inside us to lead the way to this most vital factor to having what we want. Here are some daily childlike attitudes we need to develop to have joy in our lives.

1. Look for things to appreciate and expand the list every day. I look at a tree and realize I have more blessings in my life than the leaves on that tree: experiences, knowledge, friends, health, and opportunities. Acknowledge your blessings and be actively grateful every day. Make gratitude-thinking a habit.

2. Completely forgive yourself and others for old matters that dim your joy.

3. Out of love, give something to someone who needs it; do so *because* you can!

4. Practice smiling. It sends a brain a message that things are really very good and can change your day.

Joy Creates Wealth

We are still talking about choices aren't we? When we make the right ones we are in the flow of the Universe's power, and we are also naturally abundant, and our abundance allows us to be free—because freedom and true wealth are the same thing. People without freedom are in poverty no matter how much money they have, while people who are free to create the lives they want are wealthy, no matter how little money they have. I had an aunt and uncle who were rich as Aladdin; but they were never wealthy because they were not free. They had spent their lives raising chickens and hating every minute of it, which means they were sure not doing their life's work! After over twenty years of feeding chickens and shoveling manure; saving nearly every cent of what they made, the city moved in around their little farm and they sold it for a fortune. Suddenly they were rich! And yet the only experience they had with wealth was in their fantasies. They never really wanted to be rich, because it would require them to think differently. Instead they *wanted to want* to be rich. Wanting to want is like chasing a rainbow for the pot of gold at its end; we never have to change and yet we can live in our fantasy of being rich. My aunt and uncle had stumbled upon the pot of gold and suddenly had all the money needed to be rich, yet they had no experience with wealth and weren't about to change their attitudes to accommodate it. Wealth was not an identity their egos were comfortable with and so their comfort zones did not expand along with their bank balance. For them, money was nothing more than a safeguard between them and the chickens. Because they didn't understand, they hoarded their money and made secretive investments which eventually all turned out bad. They died having never experienced wealth; never understanding that if they had used their money well, they could have had bountiful and fun lives.

The lesson they missed was this: We must radiate wealth in order to attract wealth. *We must be it before we can have it.* (Part three of the secret!) You may make a lot of money, but if you don't feel wealthy, the money will not be wealth. My aunt and uncle amassed a pile of money, but it was not wealth because it did nothing to change their minds about how careful they needed to be with every penny. They lived in a trailer house and ate meagerly; always afraid they would lose their money. If we want to develop lives of abundance, we must go to the top of the Triangle and choose Risk over Anxiety, we must expand our identities to those of the wealthy persons we dream of being.

The Universe has no limits on its support; the limitations are all ours. If you are following your life's mission and know yourself to be wealthy without limit, the Universe will provide you with whatever you need; without limit. You needn't figure out how the Universe will do it, or where your wealth will come from, you need only get your vision clear and be worthy of wealth; be grateful and keep moving forward. If you have been struggling with poverty issues, take your mind off the poverty and put it on your abundance, giving thanks for whatever you have and expecting it to increase. You will be pleasantly rewarded.

The reality you believe today is the reality you will perceive tomorrow. All the money you will ever need for your mission is available to you right now. The question is: Are you available to that money right now? You cannot do it without a joyful heart, yet most of us are not doing jobs we like; we are surviving, just holding on, like bugs caught in a spider's web, stressed out and allowing our spirits to be drained. Because we give up our joy for money, we think we are creating wealth, when in fact we are creating a prison. If the quest is costing us our health, (stress is the number one cause of illness) is that smart? Why not do both; let's become wealthy, take care of our loved ones and do it while experiencing pure joy.

My friend Monica once told a story about how her relatives reacted when she filed for a divorce back in the 1970s. Fed up with her alcoholic husband, tired of dealing with his drunkenness and poverty, she came to the end of her rope and walked out. The rightness of her decision was clear to Monica, even though she knew it was going to cause a major turmoil. She was called before an inquisition of her parents and in-laws who tried to verbally bully her back into the marriage. According to their religious beliefs, she was committing a terrible sin. Monica was told she was ruining her family's reputation, destroying her father's business and his standing in the community, defying the Church's laws, embarrassing her siblings, and traumatizing her children.

"But," Monica replied, "You're not hearing me. I'm happy now. I haven't been happy in years!"

"Happy?" they all exploded at once, "Whoever said you were supposed to be happy? You think we're happy?"

Monica shook her head in disbelief. "No, I don't. You four are the most miserable people I've ever known! Do you really think I want to live my life the same as you? To have my children grow up with a tired, angry, miserable woman for a mother?"

Monica didn't buckle under to their pressure. She *chose joy*, she chose to expand her identity and follow the Risk path to Win. She claimed her own life back and her Universe came back into balance. She learned to love herself and to see herself as a worthy person who lived in an abundant world. She went into Real Estate and gradually true wealth has come into her life.

Through my teens I often worked two eight-hour-a-day jobs; both were hard and boring, and every day I felt like I was dying. My future looked like a lifetime of the same, it was black and empty and it terrified me. I felt trapped, I wanted to run but I couldn't abandon Mom and my brother and sisters.

I was always seeing wealthy people, driving their nice cars, living in beautiful homes, playing golf, fishing, laughing with each other at their ease. I asked myself; how did they get so lucky? How could they always be in such good humor? I was just as smart as they were; how did some get the right to win gold medals, write great books, and produce wonderful movies and art? What made them so special that they got to follow their dreams while the rest of us suffered? It was plain that most of them had never even tasted poverty; why had they been allowed to escape and not me? Was it just the curse of my family that I was made to pull someone else's plow for the rest of my life? Would I always be watching from afar as others sailed through life with freedom blowing through their souls?

The answers were hard to find. The world, it seemed, was full of fast talkers who made a fortune selling their snake-oil schemes to people like me who were looking for and easy answer to their desperation. I listened to lots of get-rich-quick artists, and lost time, effort and money; all that happened was that they got richer while I got used. It seemed like forever before I finally discovered that whatever I envision comes to me when *I stay focused on MY Vision*. (Part four of the secret!) At last I had learned to let my joy and my bliss lead me, and found my life was changing. I had to slowly discard all those old beliefs about myself that I was worthless, foolish, and destined for failure. I learned that as pure soul, I am here on a divine mission. I am intelligent and I can accomplish whatever I dream of. I began to feel free and I began to feel wealthy. Because I experienced it first, and then created it, freedom, joy, and wealth came naturally to me and I healed. I was experiencing life as it is meant to be lived.

I had looked at others and envied their successes. Finally I realized that the difference between truly successful and unsuccessful people was simply this: successful people make more effective choices? By effective, I mean choices that support their visions. If day by day we stay focused on our Visions, (our passion and bliss) the Triangle will teach us how to make the best choices every time.

The Three C's of Success

Whether it is finding peace of mind, overcoming illness, having a good sex life, earning money, hitting home runs, or winning Oscars, the advantages go to those who have mastered the art of making choices and who are guided by a passion for increased joy in their lives. By following our bliss we gradually build within ourselves a foundation of three indispensable elements of self-mastery: *Clarity, Courage*, and *Confidence*. It was within those three that I found what I had searched for all those years.

Think of them as "the three C's," then please keep them in the forefront of your mind for they are the building blocks of a good life; attributes that we, as leaders, must learn and maintain. Every time we go around the outside of the Triangle these three C's expand. Clarity results from Discovery, Courage from Risk, and Confidence from Self-Love. In using the Triangle daily we increase those qualities—in every area of our lives! When we use the Triangle as routine, our Clarity, Courage and Confidence grow automatically.

Then the secret is that we are divine beings on divine missions and that we need only do the following to fulfill those missions:

- **Be accountable: Everything we experience is the result of our choices.**
- **Be grateful: Dreams can only come true when we are in joy!**
- **Be the vision: We must be it before we can have it.**
- **Be persistent: Whatever I envision comes to me when I stay focused on it.**

CHAPTER FIVE

THE TRIANGLE
IN ACTION

◇◇◇◇◇◇

We have seen examples of how each choice we make either sends us deeper into self-doubt or makes us joyful. Now let's expand our knowledge and skill level so it becomes even easier to make those good choices. The more we practice making positive, life-affirming choices at each corner of the Triangle; the more fun and abundant our lives will become. Self-doubt is a habit that, over time, becomes a part of one's self-identity. Then ego, which is threatened by change, protects that identity. But ego has no investment in making us losers. It simply protects what it knows. Then let's teach it to see us in a different light and have it protect that new positive identity. We sooth the ego and get it to support our visions by constantly walking the Triangle.

The Vision is boss but the Mission plan will readjust many times as we travel toward the Vision. We must feel free; we cannot change and learn and grow without the freedom to do so. We have seen that when we hold a vision clearly in our minds and keep focused on it with a sense of joy and confidence, a line of magnetic attraction is set up between us and that which we wish to actualize. Then our success is virtually assured. One must be wealthy in mind before one can become wealthy in wallet.

We can apply that principle to things other than money as well: One must be joyful in order to create joy, one must be successful in order to create success, and one must be loveable in order to create being loved. Here's the good news: We don't have to go out and get those identities, they are already within us. We merely give them a voice and let them come alive. The more they expand, the easier the process of attaining their rewards becomes. Again, the way to accomplish that self-expansion is by following the outside of the Triangle.

Relationships

Our relationship with others is the key to success because alone we can accomplish nothing. We rely on the support of others in every area of our lives. It is by building strong, accountable relationships with those who support our visions that we make our goals possible in ways we could never have by ourselves. Let's look at ways of strengthening relationships by using the Triangle, from *Rest* to *Discovery* to *Change* to *Risk* to *Win* to *Self-Love*.

I met Anne, (not her real name) in a seminar. Let's watch how, by using the Triangle, she climbed out of a sense of helplessness and learned to create what she wanted, step by step. When I first met her, Anne had been pretty well beaten down by life. She had worked hard and failingly to create a healthy relationship with her husband, Frank. She was tired and feeling helpless and on the verge of giving up her marriage. She had run out of ideas and out of patience.

Beginning at Rest, Anne took a look back over her life and recognized what she had accomplished. It wasn't easy, because she was still critical of herself and angry at Frank. In Rest, our entire life experience is the result of our choices; without that sense of accountability, nothing else makes sense. Understanding this, she began to see how her choices had actually been good ones in some areas of the relationship, and not so good in others. Seeing this gave her confidence because she saw clearly that the result of her choices were the experiences she was living with. This realization awakened a flicker of confidence within her and she was ready to start around the Triangle. In this journey she would focus on the vision of making her marriage a good one. She would find herself making choices that would either determine that she would have what she wanted or would fail.

Her first choice was between Discovery and Avoidance. If she chose Discovery, she would be working to improve her relationship with Frank. She could already see that going in that direction would be difficult and she might have to make changes within herself, but she had already been in Avoidance and Boredom and was not going there again if she could help it.

Anne chose Discovery and began looking for ways to make things work with Frank. It seemed overwhelming; there were so many facts, memories and confusion to sort through. She realized she needed to clearly define a specific goal and stay focused on it. She needed a Vision.

What is My Vision?

Visualizing is vital to the success of any project; if we cannot see it we cannot have it; it is as simple as that. If you decide to take a trip and don't have a destination, you can wander around the country for days and never be satisfied. A vision you can see and then commit to is an intention and it unlocks the power of the Universe, which builds a magnetic line of attraction between your vision and you. As you remain focused on your vision, that line of attraction grows stronger and pulls you to your destination. But, unless we get a vision and hold it, we cannot expect that universal support. So your vision cannot be a vague idea or a fantasy of what you want. It must be something so clear and well defined and exciting that you are willing to change yourself if necessary in order to get it; it must be a vision of your soul. The joy of its presence must inspire you so deeply that it can be felt, tasted and touched. Like a child envisioning a new red bike for their birthday, it must be something you focus your life on. It is that feeling that will keep you on track.

In clarifying a vision we ask: "What is my true intention?" or "What do I intend to create?" My intention and my vision must be exactly the same thing and we must be honest about it. We may not have always had a vision in our lives, but we have always had intention and that intention led to choices that created our reality, whether good or bad. Sometimes our intention comes from our needs to suffer, or our needs to inflict suffering, or our needs to maintain an old identity; to be right, at any cost. Sometimes our intention is to avoid making any decisions. But even then the results are ours and we are entirely accountable for them. Sometimes our intentions are drifting from one thing to another so often that nothing solid ever gets created. We can tell when our intentions are drifting, because we say we want one thing but continue to get varied results. When she understood this about intention, Anne recognized how she had been creating her own reality with Frank; she stopped seeing herself as a victim and started seeing herself as the creator of her reality.

How often have we said, "Hey, look at this mess. How the heck did this happen?" But think about it; who was driving our lives? Who was at the wheel? Who is in charge of our lives? Did we clarify what we really wanted and then focus our intentions there? Or did we just get in the back seat and let fate drive our lives? If we are at sea and leave the helm to go take a nap and the tide takes our boat onto the rocks, who is accountable? The tide?

So, in order to know what your intentions have been in any area of your life, you really only need look at your results. They tell you in a moment what your intentions were, or whether you lacked intention and let someone else run your life. Remember; vision and intention must be the same thing. *Envision* only what you intend to create and *intend* to create only what you envision, and then the power of the Universe is at your service.

The acceptance of accountability is the realization that nothing in your universe is creating your life but you. By admitting that your life has always been your own creation and always will be, you are allowing yourself to experience complete personal power and personal freedom. Such clarity is sometimes difficult because we are too close to the messes in our lives and have a battery of excuses proving we were helpless when creating them and powerless to change them. Then, like Anne, we need an objective viewpoint from friends who are willing to be honest with us. The feedback of Anne's support team was like they were holding up a mirror for her to see her truth. Armed with that knowledge, she made new choices. She saw she was not finished with her relationship; that she still had intentions and that she could make them come true. "I want to start over with Frank. I want to really listen, to really care, to laugh and play and support my husband." As that vision became clear she got excited. Remember, if we can't get excited about our vision, it cannot be our intention. Anne's excitement transformed her fear into usable energy. That is how it happens; when you are really excited about your vision, your fear becomes creative energy!

Anne wrote her vision out again and again until it was crystal clear. *My relationship with Frank is becoming more loving every day.*

You may be interested to know that of people who *do not* write their goals, less than fifteen percent ever attain them! So if you are really committed to your vision you must get it down on paper. The act of writing is an act of commitment; a written goal instantly becomes a contract between you and the creative Universe. No wonder then, that we are sometimes reluctant to write our visions, because in writing them, we turn on the engines of destiny and change our lives forever! So it takes courage to clarify your vision and write it into a contract. When you have done so, put it up somewhere, like a mirror, where you must see and read it several times every day.

Through years of experience I've discovered that when we write our visions, thoughtfully, five times every day, we even further assure them coming true because the power of our creative intention stays even more completely focused. Each time we write a vision we see it and see how our game plan on that day may need to be adjusted.

What is My Mission?

As she focused on her Vision, Anne soon came to realize that a main problem between her and Frank was her need to always be right and to be in charge. She saw she would have to get herself out of the way and start being there for him; asking questions about his thoughts and really listening. She needed to overcome her habit of correcting him because every time she did, she invalidated him and drove him away. But that would be hard for her because she had been an "editor" of others thoughts nearly all her life. Anne had always been proud of her ability to see truth. People like Frank, who sometimes made statements that were, to her mind, not absolutely accurate, needed to be corrected. When Frank was wrong she felt obligated to set him straight. To do otherwise, she had believed, was to be untrue to herself.

This is a common failing in relationships; thinking that others must agree with us before we can love them. We don't make space for them to be who they are; instead we need them to be more like us. Anne believed herself to be a seeker of truth; when anything untrue raised its sticky head, she felt she had a right and a duty to whack it off. During the seminar Anne realized that identity of herself as her sense of perfection; everything had a certain order and it was her job to see that it was maintained. In order to do that, she had often invalidated Frank's viewpoint. Now she realized that might be the reason he had almost stopped having conversations with her; he was tired of being edited and just wanted to be loved as he was. This was a hard truth for Anne to accept, but it was one that needed to be accepted before she could go on.

We often do exactly what Anne was doing; invest our creative powers in validating our beliefs instead of in following our souls' missions. We make *being right* more important than *being loved*. We lose our most valuable relationships because of it. We'll check back with Anne in just a moment to see how her mission is faring, but first let's look at a striking illustration of how erroneous viewpoints can be.

A Dark and Sinister Tale

The slender, sharply featured man, darkly dressed so as to avoid detection, armed with a gun and his favorite ripping knife, has been sliding from shadow to shadow stalking his prey all evening. Now, hearing his victim's gentle snoring, he slips into his room and up to the bed. Quietly, before the man can awaken, he crams a pillow over his face and slashes his throat from ear to ear. He holds the lunging body still until it moves no more, then quickly searches the room until he spots what he has come for; a very valuable prize. His boss will be pleased.

Smiling in the darkness, he tucks it securely into his coat and moves back toward the open window through which he entered.

But before he can duck out the window, the bedroom door is thrown wide, and in the blinding stab of light, a woman enters and stops. He freezes, trapped. The woman looks toward the blood-soaked bed, and opens her mouth as if to scream. Without hesitation, he lifts the barrel of his silenced gun and kills her with two quick bullets; one in the heart and the other in the head. Before her limp body hits the patterned carpet, he is gone and, but for the curtain blowing softly in the moonlight, the room has fallen still.

Yuk! What an awful, terrible story! This man is a cold-blooded murderer who butchers people for profit isn't he? He has probably killed many times and will again unless he is stopped. But wait! Before we strap him into an electric chair, there is more to this story. Our killer is not a deranged killer; he is a well-trained soldier who was sent by his government to recover the stolen formula to a dangerous biological weapon. Rather than being arrested as a monster, he will receive a medal for his bravery.

"Ah, then," we think. "So the man in the bed was the bad guy! Well then, for stealing a weapon to kill thousands of people, he deserved what he got!"

But wait! The fellow in the bed wasn't a terrorist; he was actually a kind and compassionate scientist who had stolen this formula to destroy it. He believed it was the only way to keep the world safe.

Then what of his poor wife who came into the room? Well, we are wrong again; she was not his wife; she was a terrorist, also after the formula so her group could use it to terrorize other countries.

Then who is right? Maybe no one, or everyone, it depends entirely on how we view it. And so much of life is like that: not one way or another, but many ways at the same time. Depending upon who is looking at a situation, right and wrong keeps shifting doesn't it? This example is purposefully dramatic, but it illustrates the point that, where several of us are seeing truth differently, none may be completely right or wrong, and the truth will often be greater than the sum of our collected viewpoints. Since effective missions are those based on truth, we must strive to be objective and keep our viewpoints flexible, allowing that *Truth is What Is*, not what we think or wish it to be. Anne had come to understand that her viewpoints might be no more valid than anyone else's; they were precious to her just because they were hers and validated her beliefs, her memories. But they often invalidated those of others. Anne didn't want to argue anymore, she didn't care about being right, she just wanted to be loved.

Anne decided to keep a journal for thirty days in which she would monitor and record her conversations and her mind chatter. From that journal she would see objectively how she was progressing, and would also have something to show her Support Team. Then she talked with friends who she trusted and who were committed to supporting her. Together they set up periodic meetings to help her stay clear and focused.

Who is on My Support Team?

Why is a support team necessary? It's necessary because the ego holds us in our same old thinking patterns, especially when it is faced with change. We become confused, distracted, dejected, feel helpless and cannot any longer see the vision. That's when the support team members step in and get us back on track. I have sometimes gotten myself into such stressful situations I can no longer remember exactly what my vision is or how important it is; I'm fighting small problems instead of looking at the big picture. I may lose sight of how often I have won against all odds and begin to feel like I am failing. That is when a member of my support team will bring me back to reality, settle me down and get my attitude readjusted.

Also, support team members can introduce us to people we need for our missions, help arrange finances or baby-sit or house tend or a myriad of other duties. But if we are receiving from them, we must be giving as well; Support Teams do not last long when they are one-sided. There are Support Teams who have been meeting regularly for over twenty years. The stories of their successes are wonderful.

What is My Next Step?

Anne was at the top of the Triangle and about to take her first step in changing her life. She knew now that it had to be a small step, one she felt she could accomplish. She would not change her entire life in one move. From her counselor, she learned that the best way to cure a habit is to replace it. Anne committed to thirty days of listening to Frank and her friends without correcting them. She would make the necessary attitudinal changes within herself to accomplish that. She would listen, she would love Frank as he was and not try to change him. Her first stumbling block was her fear that she would become someone she would not know. It was a fear that could easily have become anxiety, but Anne looked at the Triangle and realized she would be expanding, not changing her self image, and she relaxed. Anne chose Risk, committed to her thirty day mission and began expanding her identity to include one that would bring her to her vision.

How do we expand? We expand like trees; if we look at the rings of a tree that was cut down; we will find areas where old injuries, dry winters, forest fires and long lost limbs were grown over. As we expand we do not lose our old identities, rather we incorporate their wisdom and grow around them. Again, the growth rings on a giant tree are each small—small steps! We can create almost anything if we do it a step at a time, focused on each step we are taking and knowing it will lead us home.

When we understand that taking these risks is exciting rather than threatening, we lose nothing except the shackles that have kept us trapped. If Anne had not taken the Risk and had let her Fear deteriorate into Anxiety, she would have been inside the Triangle, in Paralysis and on a downward escalator where all decisions are being made for her.

The Risk Side of the Triangle is the Action Side.

There are two key elements in the process of bringing our visions into reality; commitment and action. We may want something to happen, imagine it happening, even may pray it happens. But until we take action to make it happen, the Universe sleeps. One of the most amazing words in the English language is *will*. There is power in such phrases as; "I will, you will, I am willing, we are both willing, when we are willing, it will happen." Power is diluted and intention is lost when we say "I can't, I don't know how, it's hopeless, they won't let me," or even, "I wish it could be." *Willing* changes all that, it says something is inevitable; that it *will* happen. The power does not come from the word itself, but from the place inside us that is transformed when the word is said. Will and intention are the two parts of commitment, which may be our most powerful creative tool.

A few years ago I witnessed an unforgettable example of willpower in action. It was a sunny spring afternoon in Northern Canada. My friend Ben, fishing alone in his canoe, had failed to notice that he was drifting close to where the lake flowed out into a river.

Suddenly a large fish took his lure and swam under the canoe. With-out thinking, Ben leaned over to free his line, and before he knew it, he was in the water. He was a good swimmer and wasn't wor-ried until he saw that he was being pulled into the mouth of the river where giant rapids pounded and leapt into the air. Watching in shock, we on the shore saw what was happening but were powerless to help Ben.

As he was swept into the river, Ben glanced downstream and saw a sight he would never forget: he was fast approaching white churning waves as tall as houses. He didn't know if he could survive the rapids, but he knew that just beyond the rapids were waterfalls. He knew that if the rapids didn't kill him, he would certainly die when he was swept over the falls.

The water became wild around him, roaring, leaping over jum-bled boulders. He was swimming as hard as he could against the cur-rent, but was being swept backwards as if his efforts were nothing. At that moment Ben might have panicked, might have thought: "Well, this is it; no use trying to fight this, I'm going to die. I'll never see my family again!" If Ben had allowed that voice to take over, he would have been cast into the inside of the Triangle and lost the power to save himself. With the roaring rapids just ahead and the falls coming fast, Ben knew his first plan would be his only one.

Ben had been using the Triangle for so many years; it was second nature for him to risk through fear, to find a vision and stay focused on it. So consistently had he chosen the path on the outside of the Triangle, he didn't have to think about it, his mind and body automat-ically went there. He was immediately fired with determination and began looking for a vision.

As he entered the rapids, he got a look at the nearest shore. Along that bank, a small pine tree leaned over the water. Immediately after the tree was the falls. Ben knew if he went past the tree he was dead, so the tree became his vision. Holding the small leaning tree in his mind, he swam hard, his body angled against the current as he had learned in river rafting.

He had a long way to swim and not much time to do it, but Ben was committed and his intention was clear, his willpower as fierce as the current that was flying him toward death. His great fear had become great energy and he completely trusted the Great Spirit of Life that was coursing through him. He did not plead for his life; his prayers were expressed in action and determination. He knew the odds against him were overwhelming; but he never lost faith, never considered failing.

Waves crashing over his head made it nearly impossible to catch a breath, but his fear pushed him on with fewer breaths, swimming as he had never swum before, holding always in his mind that one vision: the small pine tree where he would climb out of the river. As he was dragged toward the falls, he was tossed about like a small stick by waves roaring around him so high he could not see beyond them. But he knew that he was moving downstream much too fast, and that unless something changed, he could not make it to his tree. That is when Ben's commitment was tested. It was the moment of give-up or give-all. In a rage, Ben became even more determined, a fresh flood of energy poured into his body and he discovered a whole new dimension of himself; strength he never knew.

With his arms stroking like propellers and his feet flying, he was spun around and sucked under. There, to his amazement, he saw a large trout swimming along the river bottom. As he swept by the fish, he noticed that it was barely fighting the current at all. It turned and watched him go by. Ben's head bobbed up and he saw the shore only ten yards away, but his small tree was parallel with him now which meant he was already entering the tongue of the falls. He saw that no matter how hard he would swim now, it could not save him. The tree would pass before he got to it.

Yet giving up was not in him. At each stage, as the pull of the river had increased, his intention had increased too; his commitment was clearer and his will more absolute. Now the river gathered itself for the plunge over the falls which were only feet away. The mist blotted out his vision and the roar filled his ears.

At this point, many of us would have weakened, have given up and surrendered to the terrible inevitable. To do so would have been natural and completely understandable, but Ben was not finished, was not about to give up his life on this day. And into that moment, hanging on the precipice of the falls, came a joy, a joy that illuminated his whole being and the splendid ferocity with which he now poured the last of himself into the fight. The joy was life at its purest; he was alive, more alive than he had ever been.

He was a bare ten feet from where the water curled over the falls, and he was dragged now into the smooth, fast apron of water just before the river leaped into space. Ben had not forgotten his vision his small leaning pine tree. It was still the only reality in his mind but now he needed something to grab, something to keep him from being flung over the falls. Without thinking he dove to the bottom. His feet were being sucked into the falls as he grabbed a rock on the bottom. He expected the force of the water to be enormous against his grip, but to his amazement, the current there was almost gentle. Then he remembered the trout lazing over the rocky bottom and realized that along a river bottom must be a natural eddy, a slowing of water! Holding his breath and hand over hand, he pulled himself across the bottom of the river toward his tree. Near shore the eddy actually pushed him forward.

Ben crawled out of the river exactly where he had envisioned himself landing; right in front of his tree!

Later I talked to Ben about his experience and asked him what it had done for him.

"I realized that when I can't get something I'm after, it's either because I don't see it clearly enough, or because I'm not really determined. It is a lesson I am so grateful for. And, what about the strength you showed? I didn't know I had that in me. Yet, I must tell you that there is only one thing that saved me and it is this: my absolute determination to go all out. I mean all-out!"

I saw the blaze of fury in his eyes as he said it and knew he was feeling it again, that magnificent surge of willpower that pushed him through the rapids.

"I will treasure this experience for the rest of my life. I changed today; I am not the same guy who fell in the river."

Like Ben, when our goals seem impossible, that is when we must intensify our determination even more; that's when we learn who we really are. Then we learn that we can work miracles, that there is no limit to the amount of power available to us if we have the courage to claim it.

On her sixth birthday, my wife, Mary, was given a packet of certificates for free ice cream at her favorite fountain. But because her big brothers always took her things, she hid them. It was not until twelve years later, when moving out of her old bedroom, that she finally found the certificates but by then, the ice cream fountain had long since gone out of business. We are given opportunities every day to win and win big. If we hide them away, if we save them they become as worthless as Mary's leftover ice cream certificates.

How often have we hoped and prayed, done our affirmations and held a good vision, but got no result because we took little or no

action? Our visions cannot be accomplished with half-hearted ges-
tures. To overcome the obstacles to getting what we want, we need
the power of intention and will.

When asked by a reporter her secret to winning marathons,
Mickey Gorman, a champion long-distance runner, said she makes
sure she has absolutely nothing left when she crosses the finish line.
Then, in each race she often finds she has more than she had in the
last race. Like Mickey Gorman, we can reach beyond ourselves in
times of need, and when we do, we will find new depths of wisdom
and power. If we lose life's marathon, it will not be because we were
destined to lose, but because we did not dare to push beyond our limits. And then we lose more than the race; we lose the chance to know
who we really are.

As we go forward with our missions, always walking the Triangle,
we become more and more confident, not only in ourselves, but in the
power that is available to us from the Universe. While we are learning
that lesson, we must not give up because no matter how impossible
the goal seems, there is always a way to win.

I am Expanding My Identity

In this phase you must come to realize who you are on a higher level
than before. You are challenging yourself to be stronger and more
deliberate and that means expanding your concept of who you are.
When you are challenged, as you will be, in this Risk side of the Triangle, you must constantly think of yourself as the "new you" and not
let the old you make your decisions. In order to do that, consider who
you would be if your vision was behind you, already accomplished.
That is who you must allow yourself to be now. There is a funny old
saying that "you can't get there from here." In this case it is true; you

feel wealthy before you can become wealthy; not by spending money you don't have, but by thinking as wealthy people do; especially about money. You must be healthy in your mind before you can become healthy in your body. You must be loveable before you can find someone to love you. Like every step of the Risk side of the Triangle, this will often feel uncomfortable because your ego does not easily let go of its old identity. It tries to keep you focused on who you have been rather than who you are becoming. This is where clarity, courage and commitment come in. Just keep your mind on the Vision and allow your soul's wisdom to guide you.

Affirmations

To expand our identities, we find that affirmations are tools we cannot do without.

When joined with good intentions and consistent actions, affirmations overcome and eventually convert old thinking patterns. You can begin now by designing affirmations that will empower your personal expansion. Examples are: *I am free. I am experiencing complete wealth. I am totally healthy. I am a lovable and loving (man or woman). I feel others liking and appreciating me.* These are only a few suggestions, yet they are ones that have proven effective for others. Do you see how, if you made them a constant mental message, they might transform your self-identity?

To be effective, affirmations must be done with as much focus as possible. I recommend fifty times four times a day for thirty days. Consecutive days are very important, so if you miss a day, please go back to day one and start again. Affirmations may be oral or written or both. If you are repeating them orally or in your mind, I suggest you count them on your fingers, using first the left hand for ten and then the right hand for ten and so on. In this way you engage both sides of your brain in the empowering process. For the first ten days or so, you may be doing these affirmations not believing there is a chance in the world they are true, but don't give up. At about fifteen days you may begin to think it is possible, changes are now happening! At about twenty or twenty-five days, you are growing into your new identity, yet the affirmations begin to seem meaningless; like saying "the sky is blue, the sky is blue." It is at this point many people quit, but it is a mistake because, though the mind is now accepting this new truth, the old identity has not yet been replaced. So keep going until your new neuronal pathways are paved and anchored. During this process you must also make behavioral changes so that your actions become consistent with the new identity. For example if you are now seeing yourself as being in the flow of abundance, you may no longer allow yourself to get down because your bills are not paid, you must adopt the attitude that this financial problem is temporary and that you are in the process of ending it. You must act in ways that validate and help establish your new sense of yourself. Needless to say, the rewards of self-pity and having others sympathize with your poverty are rewards you must now forgo.

Anne's vision of having a good relationship with Frank, her husband, required her to expand her identity in several ways. Her first challenge was to become an interested and active listener. She was beginning to see her lifetime of experiences in a new way. Things looked different because her filters were changing. The new world she was discovering had infinite possibilities.

Until now, Anne had thought she was controlling things, had thought it was she who was in charge. Now she realized it was not her, but her ego that had been running her life. Her ego (memories and beliefs) acted like a despotic reference librarian ripping from all incoming books any pages not conforming to what she had already experienced. Our egos are subtle, complex, and powerful enough to fool us into thinking anything is true or untrue. People die daily defending what their egos say is right. Remember, your ego would rather you die than for it to change its attitude. You cannot allow this tyranny; you are a soul on a divine mission, you created your body and mind and made your ego CEO of that corporation. If it now refuses to serve your divine needs, fire it and hire one that will.

Anne knew she would never have stepped beyond the boundaries set by her ego without the guidance of the Triangle. Using it she was able to discover within her, a peace and a confidence she had never felt before. She had broken the old mold of her identity and discovered a bright new relationship with the world.

Is it difficult? Yes, it is difficult because difficulty is the nature of life. Some may disagree because they want life to be easy. But that is not to be; life is a challenge and challenges are difficult. Examples; The World Series, The Boston Marathon, The Super Bowl, The World Cup, painting scenery, sculpting, building a home, starting a business, raising children, losing weight—life is difficult! But these are the challenges that make life a joy. How would life be without them? Anne hoped Frank would wake up and grow with her; but if he did not, she was going on anyway. She had found a path that empowered and rewarded her every day. She was in joy and she was living free.

I Am Focused On My Vision

I must expand in order to come into alignment with my vision, but expanding my identity can become almost impossible if I am trying to expand it from the same ego-consciousness that anchors the old one. We will know where our creative *intention* is by seeing where our *attention* is. I cannot, for example, acquire wealth while seeing myself as poor, nor find a good relationship while seeing myself as unlovable, nor create perfect health while believing myself to be ill. I cannot get to the vision while focused on obstacles to the vision. I must keep my attention on the vision itself and allow the creative intention to focus accordingly.

Chinese Rivers

Flying over China I saw something that really changed my thinking; I saw rivers winding their way between countless mountains on their way to the sea. It occurred to me that if a river at its inception as a small spring were to ask: "Who am I and where am I going?" The answer might be: "Your understanding of who you are will come to you on your journey." In every step you are becoming you. You, the river, are going home to the sea. We can see then, why a river, which ultimately belongs in the sea, will start as a spring in the mountains, thousands of miles away, and flow through many difficulties to get back home. The same quest is that of our souls; each placed strategically distant from their goals so that as they travel back to their source, they define themselves and expand in wisdom and joy. Every obstacle, then, is a teacher that increases me and shows me more of who I am.

The river is powered on its journey to the sea by gravity–around this mountain and through that valley and always onward—being pulled by the relentless force of gravity. Our souls are being pulled by a force just as powerful and just as relentless. This magnetic attraction is pure grace. It pulls our fledgling souls along their paths, through valleys of doubt and mountains of difficulty. Every win, every vision that is fulfilled along the way, brings us closer into alignment with Nature's Law, or God's Law or Great Spirit's Law; (the same by any name). Eventually, matured and ready to step up to the next greater dimension in our eternal journey, we arrive at the Sea of Oneness.

You are reading this not by accident, but because it is time for you to see that every doubt, every obstacle that stops you from following your true vision is a falling from grace; a crippling of your soul on its journey to freedom. When you realize your vision and move toward it, you must do so with clarity, commitment and courage (the three C's). You must be aware of how to overcome the obstacles that sap your faith and divert your trust. You must believe and know that there is *always a way* to overcome the obstacles between you and your Destination. This is knowledge you will gain step by step when you keep in mind that you are a divine being on a divine mission, being pulled along your path by grace. You will learn it from your Universe if you are listening with your soul, you will learn it from your support team and from your accomplishments. You will find that no power in the Universe can resist or turn aside the force of grace. With this powerful magnet pulling you even as gravity pulls the river to the sea, and as Ben was pulled from his river, you need do only two things; stay focused on your vision and take the necessary and appropriate actions called for by your mission. Sometimes taking the appropriate actions simply means *showing up*, mentally, physically and emotionally, and then trusting the river to carry you.

I Am Working My Mission

Expanding our identities always opens new avenues of opportunity we didn't see before. As our identities become flexible, we learn to stop defending old patterns and allow new opportunities to appear where we only saw problems before. With every new problem comes an opportunity to change the rules of the game; like making lemon pie from lemons instead of cursing their sourness. Our missions are the paths to our visions and must be flexible. Carl's situation is a good example of how expanding a viewpoint empowers a mission.

Carl is a manufacturer of shoes. A few years ago he found himself stuck with tens of thousands of pairs of sport shoes that had gone out of style. He had an enormous amount of money tied up in this inventory which was taking up vital space in his warehouse. He had considered shipping the shoes to a foreign country, selling them at a discount, or recycling them, ideas that would cost him money and possibly injure the prestige of his name. But what to do with fifty thousand pair of shoes?

Then Arlan, one of my most successful graduates who now works as a success coach, talked to Carl about expanding his viewpoint. "Think in a new way!" he told him. "Let yourself get a little crazy. Let the unthinkable come to you and write it down. Don't turn away any idea before you've completely considered it."

After brainstorming with Arlan for a while, Carl suddenly discovered that he had been hung up on getting the most *money* out of his overstocked inventory rather than the most *value*. They are often not the same. He got really excited. "Value!" he yelled. "That's what I'm really after here . . . value!"

Carl realized he had been too close to the situation to sort it out, which is why we need support teams and success coaches. He saw that he had shoes with a value to the world that had nothing to do with money, and that if he were able to properly release that value to the world, it might come back to his company multifold. And it would get rid of the shoes! So Carl decided that through nonprofit organizations he would distribute the shoes free as rewards to young people all over America who were serving as community-service volunteers. In return he would receive a tax credit for his donation, lots of publicity and goodwill from the media, and the great feeling of having contributed to a good cause. In the long run he might even make more money than if he had sold the shoes.

Arlan had helped Carl challenge his old belief system about how things must be done. In the process he expanded his creativity-comfort zone. Like Carl, when we get stuck in our old definitions of ourselves and the reality around us, we don't see new options when they arise. This is the kind of risk the Triangle advocates, one that opens our eyes to new realities and opportunities.

Historically, most solutions to problems are reaction-fixes that only make bigger problems. Carl would have just made new problems for himself if he sold his overstocked shoes at a discount. He might have solved the problem of excess and obsolete stock and brought in money, but in the process he would have put shoes on retail shelves that competed with his full-priced ones. He would have alienated his retailers and jeopardized his company's marketing program. By following his old thinking patterns, Carl's solution might have created bigger problems than it solved.

The idea of selling his shoes at a discount would have been a reaction-fix, and would have surely created more complications. The solution he chose was an opportunity-fix because it opened new opportunities. Arlan's theory, whether in business or personal life, is, "Don't try to dissolve the problem, turn it into an opportunity!"

Carl and Anne both grew as persons, they expanded their viewpoints. Not without fear; but because of fear. They learned that fear is pure energy and that how we use it determines whether it helps or harms us. Whether it is fear of failing, fear of rejection, fear of the unknown, or fear of anything else, having a vision and using fear as energy will help us transform problems into opportunities and move on. Without fear we could not grow.

Some might ask: "Why did Anne have to do all the changing in her relationship with Frank? Why couldn't she demand that he do some changing, too?"

Here is a three-part answer to those questions.

1. My grandpa, who was the last of the great American cowboys and smart as a whip, used to tell me, "To get a horse to go the direction you want, you first have to ride him in the direction he is going." Grandpa was right. The best way to win an argument is to align with your opponent, get him going your way and then steer him your way. Frank might go in Anne's direction if he was first able to make his points and feel them validated.

2. The problem Anne was solving was hers, not Frank's. We have already seen that she created hers by the choices she made. When she decided she wanted a new life, she made new choices. If we want tomorrow to be different than today, we must make different choices today than we did yesterday. Anne expanded beyond her need to be right in order to get what she wanted. She shed the self-image that been creating her problem.

3. Anne was growing in self-confidence and grace by making changes. She was no longer stagnated by her relationship. She was taking charge of her life, claiming responsibility for her choices. Whether Frank came around or not, whether they decided to have a loving relationship or go their separate ways, Anne was winning, because she was expanding her own life.

I Am Contributing

When we are living as we should: following our life's missions, we are a natural part of the flowing Universe. As such, we are contributors to the ecology of life on every level; such is the wondrous magic of Creation. In the human family, we are all contributors to the whole as we follow our missions. We influence others; provide services, products and security and opportunities for others. We set standards for living that allow those who follow us to have options they would never have experienced. If you think back to when you were a child, in growing up you will remember certain adults who influenced you, whom you admired and respected. To some degree each of them has helped form your sense of what life and living should be. We are like six billion plus pieces of a jigsaw puzzle, when your piece fits with those around you, you help complete the picture for all now and all ages to come. The ARAS Foundation gives an Annual Ripple Award to someone who has, by following his or her life's work, made a ripple in the pond of the Universe. Such ripples go out, and out, touching and uplifting the lives of those around them, and the lives of those not yet born.

There is a reason this is the last step before **Win**; it is because acknowledging that you make a difference is important for what is about to come.

From Win to Self-Love

Anne has arrived at the corner of the Triangle labeled **Win**. In Win we acknowledge what we have accomplished and how we have grown and changed. Anne is about to make the third of the three choices that are to determine the course of her life. She has already chosen **Discovery** over **Avoidance** and **Risk** over **Anxiety**; now she must decide between **Self-Love** and **Unworthiness**. Here is how she might weigh arguments for and against accepting herself as a winner:

For: She will gain confidence and clarity and new opportunities will
   open for her.

For: She will finally be in charge of her life.

For: She will become a positive influence and inspiration to those she loves.

For: Her entire life will begin changing for the better.

Against: Some might say she needs to be more humble.

Against: She might feel pressured to keep winning which may be scary.

Against: She once had a hiding place inside the Triangle, not much was expected of her and she could get away with being spiritually lazy. If she is truly a winner, how can she ever go back?

This is a vital place of choice because when we reach **Win**, if we deny our new identities, the clarity and courage we have earned will be swept away in a blink and our risks will have been for nothing. Our old identity will have limited everything we accomplished. But in walking around the Triangle we have created new identities that are more clear, committed and courageous than ever before. Our trust for ourselves and our Universe has expanded. We experience life now with a new clarity, commitment and courage. If we accept these wins and ourselves as winners, we will dilute any remaining identities of unworthiness and begin building new identities that will transform our lives.

Win and **Self-Love** are places to *express* what those Triangle experiences were for us. It is very important to express, because experiences not expressed, either have no benefit to us, or in cases like Post Traumatic Stress Disorder, become blocks to our self-realization. Unless life flows into us as experience and out of us as expression we cannot benefit from life. It is in the act of expressing that we integrate experiences into our souls and allow them to become wisdom. And if we are not vision-oriented in our sharing, if we do not keep in mind that we are vibrating with the Universe, we may lose our balance and fall from grace. How will Anne think of her **Win**? Her choices range from *Victim* ("I could have done better!") to *Victor:* ("I did my and it was good enough!") By accepting herself as a winner she allows a new self to emerge.

Let's look at what happened to a hardworking man named Jake who tried for years to buy a farm. Every time he got the money for the down payment, one of his kids got sick, his car broke down, or something else happened that drained away his savings. By working all one summer, driving a truck during the daytime and working as a watchman at night, he finally made it. In October, he paid the money and moved his family onto the farm.

His wife, Betty, was rightfully proud of him. "Jake, look at what you've done! Everyone said you were a just dreamer that you'd never really get your own farm, and now here you are. You did it! You're one amazing guy!"

But Jake still didn't trust that it would last, he was sure it would all fall apart if he believed in it. So he didn't anchor his **Win**. He brushed it off saying, "Well, I could have done it years ago. As it is, I only barely made it because I got some good jobs last summer."

It would have been smart for Jake to anchor his **Wins** and bank all the self-confidence he could, because hard times were coming and he would need it. But he thought himself humble and good because of his modesty and expected God to reward him for his humility. He didn't talk about how he had overcome his fears and how excited and thrilled with himself he had been when he first realized he was going to get his farm. Jake felt unworthy of that identity.

When his crops failed for the first two years, Jake wasn't surprised; "I thought it would all fall apart," he told his wife. "This is why I told you not to get so excited about things."

But what had Jake done to himself? He had starved his soul and fell from grace. Now he must fight through his troubles with no help from his God. It was the same crippled consciousness he'd fought through to get the farm in the first place. He was starting over, his meager self-confidence blown away in the dust storms. He figured it made sense because it matched the identity of himself he had always known; everything he had ever done had been hard and filled with failure. Why should this be any different?

What had really frightened Jake about accepting his win was this: he thought that between his old image as a failure and his new image as a winner was a space where he would have neither. What he didn't know is that there is no such space, when he really let go of being a poor struggling failure, his new identity would have stepped right in. Like a kid afraid to jump over a stream, he stayed on the losing side, the side he was familiar with. If he had anchored his win, he would now have something to hang onto, something to get him through the rough times, he would have gained the three C's: **Clarity**, **Courage**, and **Confidence**.

In her experience with her husband, Frank, Anne chose to celebrate her growth. She took her best friend to lunch and told all about spending the first thirty days of total support for Frank, listening and loving him. She wrote about it daily in her journal. As she expressed herself, validating her new identity, her new viewpoint of reality, she felt herself growing stronger and more peaceful. She felt herself filling with joy.

Anne chose **Self-Love** over **Unworthiness**. She liked her new confidence and wasn't about to let it go. Then, sure enough, she found that the path of **Self-Love** was to be another challenge.

The affirmations that follow: *I am Loved—I am Blessed—I am Safe—I am Free*, together are powerful builders of personal power and self-confidence; yet there are also times when each of them needs to stand on its own or in companionship with only one other, such as: I am Blessed—I am Safe. I think that as you read them you will agree that every one of them is important to the validation of your soul, and that at times each of them will need its own place in the armament of your soul. If I awaken in the dark hours of night, flooded by feelings of insecurity or loss, I will say them in order, over and over in my mind until sleep returns. Yet even then, I may find that only one or two of them are really the ones my mind needs to hear.

I Am Loved

Here we acknowledge that we are both loved and lovable, not only by others who know us, but by the Great Spirit of Creation Itself.

We each are unique; no other beings like us were ever created and Great Spirit knows each of us individually. One may ask the purpose for music, or art, a sunset, or light reflecting on water, and the only answer can be that they are constantly flowing gifts of love to us from our Creator. If we choose to see it in this way, this is Paradise, a gift of love. We are also loved by each other. How much we are loved is often a measure of how completely we are willing to surrender to loving another. If we get into right and wrong or superior and inferior contests, we stifle love. We cannot afford those kinds of wins, because to lose joy is to fall from grace and lose Paradise. Love is the ultimate power we humans can employ. Babies who are not allowed to love and be loved, nearly always sicken and die. Those who do survive are often psychologically damaged. Diseases such as cancer and heart disease frequently find their roots in the unloved or unloving places in our bodies. Healing often takes more than medicine, when we realize that it is only through the expression and experience of love that people, and even our whole society, can be made well.

I Am Blessed

We must agree by now, having come this far in our thinking, that we are being held in the hands of Great Spirit. As pure and perfect souls on eternal journeys of enlightenment, we are given whatever we need. In recognizing how completely we are blessed, we open the doors of grace into our lives. We surrender to being guided and pulled along the avenues of our self-realization. Every experience, every relationship, every incident that ever happened, or is happening to you is a blessing if you will accept it as such. If so, it will give you joy and allow grace to flow through and romance your soul.

I Am Safe

We are being protected. How many times have we been scant seconds or inches from death or destruction and how many times have we avoided it? We are here for a reason, a divine reason and are guided, protected, surrounded with grace. Our fears are not threats, but instead are packets of energy given to overcome threats. Your insecurities and doubts will disappear as you realize you were not abandoned into this dark and mysterious world but are, at every step, being guided and illuminated with grace.

I Am Free

I am free to be me. I am free to choose the outside of the Triangle always. I am free to create my own life. I may have jobs I don't really like, but in each case I am free to choose to do them. One important part of this freedom is knowing that I am forgiven. Like Tia Maria's example of the healing that immediately happens when any part of

Nature is disrupted, we, as part of the Nature are also immediately forgiven. We, then, do not have to carry the burdens of guilt or shame, nor let them taint our self-identities. We are truly free to go forward and live our lives as we dream they can be. This freedom gives me a sense of power and of joy. I am like a child in a summer meadow, and the meadow is my life.

Back at home in Rest

At Rest, (Be) Anne was feeling a peaceful stillness and *gratitude* for all her blessings, She was aware of wisdom and strength expanding in her, revealing to her a self she had never known. Sharing with her team what she had accomplished and filled with new power and freedom, she felt as wealthy as if she had won the lottery. She looked back and remembered how she had found her Vision through Discovery; how frightened she had been in Change before she abandoned her restrictive thinking and Risked. And how, by following her mission, how she had overcome her Unworthiness and anchored her Win. And then, in joy, Anne loved herself and others on her way to *Rest*. Retracing this journey in her mind, she saw how her life had begun transforming every day.

You will discover as Anne did, that the Triangle is not flat, as on a piece of paper, but that each leg is an uphill climb so that we constantly elevate and expand ourselves as we climb; spiraling upward. In Rest, Anne was on a much higher plane, a greatly expanded state of self awareness and of consciousness, than when she was here in Rest before. She now saw ahead of her possibilities she had only fantasized before. Soon she will again face the challenges of expanding her mission and growing, but now it does not seem so frightening, it seems like an exciting adventure filled with the promise of joy. But for now, she is in Rest, just doing things that delight her, anchoring her feeling of being loved and experiencing gratitude for life. She might go to a movie or get a massage today. Maybe she'll do both!

The Danger of Not Loving Yourself

Before we leave this story, let's go back to Win for just a moment. What if Anne had not been able to overcome her tendency toward Unworthiness? What if she had not accepted herself as a winner and gone into Self-Love? What if she had instead been sucked inside the Triangle? Remember this would have been her choice; we are always at choice on the corners of the Triangle. If we don't make a positive choice to be in Self-Love then our Unworthiness automatically pulls us inside. If Anne had let that happen, we would have seen her moving from Unworthiness to Anxiety by the dark path of that spiritually corrosive duo, Guilt/Shame. She would have felt the accusations of an old program telling her she should feel guilty about being who she was, as her shame ate away at her. We all have those voices inside us, but we may not understand how destructive and inappropriate they are. Still, you might ask, "Aren't there things for which we *should* feel shame or guilt?"

It was 1975 when I first began teaching that *guilt* and *remorse* are two very different things. I had discovered that remorse was the natural, corrective pain that gets us back on the track of good ethical and moral thinking and that, after doing its good work, it evaporates. Guilt however, once it gets its tentacles wrapped around you, makes its home like a parasite in your subconscious and takes up residence in your self-identity. Unlike remorse, which tells you that you have *done* a bad thing, guilt insists *it is you* who are bad and that your deed is the natural outcome of your inherent wickedness. When that identity becomes anchored, then one's whole life must be lived in reaction rather than action, one is always expecting to be punished for being evil and can never be free to take real risks and excel at life because punishment always seems to await. There are *religious* leaders who will tell us we are inherently evil and must be saved from our evilness. However there is no evidence that any great *spiritual* leader, including Jesus, ever told us we were evil by nature. In fact, such teaching is the opposite of who He was and the life he lived.

Guilt and its ugly little stepsister, Shame, are cancers of the soul that become so entwined in our self-images, so deep-rooted, that they disempower us, weakening every part of our lives. When I first began teaching this philosophy, there was an enormous outcry against my viewpoint from religious leaders, teachers, parents, and law-enforcement personnel who were convinced that it was the "healthy" guilt and shame inside people that kept them from doing terrible things. Now, many years later, that flak has died down and most have come to realize that guilt deters neither sinner nor sin, that feelings of guilt are not only psychologically damaging, but are far more likely to cause, than to prevent, wrongdoings.

Why is this? It is because when I believe I am a *good person who has done a bad thing;* my subsequent behavior is totally different than when I believe I am a *bad person acting from that identity.* In the first, I am troubled by my remorse, reminded sharply that I am in violation of my own morality and ethics and will make amends; in the second, I am doing what seems natural for me; acting from the core of my identity as a bad person. People tend to act as they believe they are. When people, who feel they are bad, do good things, it makes them feel uneasy and they make corrections, in other words they stop doing good things and do bad things that balance their identities. When people who feel they are good do something bad, they also become uneasy and make corrections; they stop doing bad things and do good things to balance their identities. Guilt and Shame are corrosive to the kind of identities necessary to be in grace and do good work in the world. They weaken confidence; destroy souls, families, and entire nations.

Why do I say guilt is chronic? Why can't little Johnny feel only temporarily guilty and shameful for having killed the bird, and then later love himself again? The reason is simple: like all kids, Johnny largely forms his self-image from the feedback he gets from others, particularly adults. He cannot see himself except through the eyes of others and must believe what we tell him about himself. If those he respects as authorities say to him, "Johnny you are a bad boy; shame on you! You will be punished for this," we assign to him the identity of *bad boy*. But if, instead, we say, "Johnny, you're a good boy, but look now, you've done a bad thing, and you must make amends," then we are using his remorse, his sense of himself as a good person who is temporarily off track, to reinforce his moral strength. He is reminded that his nature is that of a good boy. In parenting Johnny, we do not want his mistakes to define his identity, but his growing moral identity to define and eventually dictate his behavior. Johnny will learn who he is from the feedback he gets; teach him he is stupid, he will behave stupidly; teach him he is brilliant and he will strive to perform brilliantly.

CHAPTER SIX

ARAS
REAL LOVE
IS REAL POWER

I n the last chapter we found how beneficial it was to choose Self-Love instead of Unworthiness. Self-Love, as on the Triangle, is the greatest gift one can ever experience. It is allowing you to bathe in the Universe's deepest and most nourishing energy. It is ecstasy that is beyond description, as I'm sure you know; thousands of songs and books and movies and works of art have tried in vain to capture that magic, yet it remains as illusive and hard to capture as a morning rainbow. Some things can only be experienced and love is one of them. My friend Chuck Nicklin the famous underwater photographer and I were standing on the deck of a boat out of San Diego one afternoon, watching the sunset on a stormy sea. It was a memorable moment and I was filled with joy from the scene and from being with my friend.

I said, "Chuck, why aren't you taking a picture of this?"

He smiled, "Bob, there is no way to take a picture of what we are seeing and feeling here; we have to just anchor this inside and remember it."

Thanks Chuck, I did keep it, and thirty years later it still nour-
ishes me.

Too often we think that in giving or receiving affection we are
exchanging love. While affection is a part of love, it alone cannot sustain the soul. Did you ever get a beautiful flowering plant as a gift, and
then forget to water it? Did it whither and die? Many people get mar-
ried thinking their shared affection will sustain them, but affection
is a flowering plant that requires more than just admiration if it is to
grow. By itself it is just a part of love. How many of those marriages
last? More than fifty percent of Americans get divorced because the
acceptance, respect and support never showed up and then the affection died.

One of the hats I wear is that of a Realtor, I go to a many lec-
tures and seminars to learn more about this trade and in nearly
every class the term, *relationships skill* is touted as vital to success.
It makes me uneasy to think that the purpose of developing relationships skills is to con people into doing business with me. If my
purpose for being good at relationships is just to get people's money,
am I not a prostitute?

Yet we must have good relationships skills because without them
we cannot long survive in any business, marriage or friendship. In
commerce we don't do business with fish or groceries or cars or
computers, we do business with *people*. Individual accomplishment
is a myth, everything happens by teamwork. We choose our teams
according to our identities, our beliefs about ourselves. Those used to
losing tend to choose losers as teammates, those who love winning
usually choose winners. Elton Rule took a job as salesman at an L.A.
TV station and rose to be president of ABC in less than five years.
As we were having supper one evening I asked how he accomplished

such a feat. "It wasn't too hard," he said, "I just surrounded myself with good people." Elton's rule is a good one; whether it is washing cars or selling Real Estate, every business is *people business* and recruiting a good team is vital to success. But the purpose of the relationship between me and each person on my team must be deeper than just for the success of the venture and we both must know it. The question is this; do I want my relationships to be successful because I really like this person and want to build satisfying friendships with him, or do I just want them to serve me and then get out of my way?

Every person who has ever done anything extraordinary, whether it was winning a gold medal or finding the cure for a deadly disease, had a team to thank. Even my late friend Dick Proenneke, author of One Man's Wilderness, living all alone with wolves, bears, and eagles in the heart of Alaska, kept strong, healthy relationships with members of the Park Service, with those who flew in his supplies and mail from me and others. Dick abandoned society, and then created one of his own that worked for him. Like all of us, he needed the grace that can only come through good relationships. Again, there is no such thing as solitary accomplishment; without relationships, Dick Proenneke's dream of living alone in the wilderness could not have come true.

Over the past thirty years, I have had the privilege of teaching hundreds of thousands of people how to use the acronym ARAS to create and maintain the very best relationships possible. It is easy to memorize and to use everyday and it can make you a master of relationships and even change enemies into friends. ARAS stands for **Acceptance**, **Respect**, **Affection**, and **Support**. If you make ARAS a habit and follow its simple steps in dealing with everyone, you will soon find that nearly everyone likes you and wants to help you.

ARAS

Acceptance and Respect; these two words form our attitudes about others and the world around us. We often think others cannot read our minds. If I dislike someone, I may think that if I keep smiling he will think I like him, that if I find someone rejectionable, as long as I am pleasant, he will not know it. But we are connected on a much deeper level than simple words or facial expressions; we are one soul, divided into individual incarnations. Because of this eternal connection, we can no more hide our feelings about each other than can a child hide hers from her mother. The love that flows between us is grace; it keeps us linked together and to our Creator. Many, if not most, terminal diseases are traceable to a lack of love. When babies are left in their cribs, not allowed to give love and be loved; they die. It is as simple as that. When the grace of love stops flowing between us, our souls become isolated from their Source and we begin to die physically. On the deepest level, everyone realizes that truth, which is why we strive to be close.

Acceptance

Acceptance: saying "yes" to reality, to truth, is the first step in becoming a creator. Unless we are accepting what is: truth, we are automatically rejecting what is and then have no platform from which to create. More simply put, it is like trying to paint when we do not recognize the brushes available to us, or trying to cook when we do not accept the stove upon which our meal will be cooked. Truth is the foundation of our lives and wherever reality shows up, be it positive or negative, the first step in changing it or expanding it is to accept it. The secret of most martial art disciplines is to completely accept the opposing force coming at you and then divert it past or through you in a harmless way. To reject it is to build a barrier with your body that will then get hammered. The same thing happens to your mind and emotions when you reject truth, it still comes, but it finds a wall to crash into rather than a door to go through. The strongest trees, the ones that survive hurricanes, are the ones that bend most easily. Those that will not bend, will break. When I am in resistance to truth, that resistance soaks up my energy, takes me out of the game and even paralyzes me.

How about the past? Those things that seemed to have destroyed parts of our lives? Can we change them now? No, we cannot. We cannot change the past; we can only build upon it. But how can we build upon what we reject? If truth seems like sour lemons to me, I can either shrivel from the sourness or make a lemon pie. When I accept it, I find that the sourness of life forms an important balance that I need in order to keep growing.

Each person brings a new experience into my life. If that experience seems impossible to accept, my karmic duty is to expand my identity until I can find it acceptable. I will never change that which I dislike by rejecting it. But by accepting it, I open the door to new possibilities; ways to make lemon pies. By rejecting it, I am repressing the part of myself that can grow and learn from this situation and become more powerfully creative. When we accept people the way they are, we are accepting the Universe the way it is and are then empowered by it. When we reject people, we cut off that power and lose our ability to create things new and wonderful.

The opposite of acceptance is rejection, and, whether or not we express it, people feel it. They know when they are not accepted, because even the most subtle rejection hurts. Then they protect themselves by building walls between them and us and we become their enemies.

Acceptance is an attitude, not an action; we don't have to move in with another person or have his babies to show we are accepting him; we just need to allow him to be exactly the way he is and then begin building our relationship from there.

But what if he is a monster, a murderer or molester? How can we accept that? Acceptance is not about making friends with monsters, it is about seeing truth and dealing with it as it is, not as we would like it to be. Sometimes we have to deal with harsh realities, and it is not pleasant. I have done counseling and seminars in prisons. I can still remember a certain serial killer I spent time with. He seemed to have no soul. He had absolutely no remorse for the terrible crimes he had committed. I did not like what he represented, how he thought or his lack of principles. But he was real and I had to accept his reality. When he was sentenced, I pleaded for his life, because I knew the only way we can ever end the scourge of serial killers like him in our society is to stop killing them and start studying them. The goal is to better recognize the patterns of psychopathic behavior early enough to reroute them before they take root. But how can that happen when we keep rejecting reality by exterminating it? It is like burning down a home where a murder was committed and destroying all the evidence in the process. To put it even more simply, we cannot change anything until we accept it and understand it exactly as it is. If we dislike something, then that dislike must also be accepted.

The murders had already happened, and so were truth, a part of this reality. My rejection of them would not have changed them one whit. In order to go forward with my life, I must deal with truth as it is. Hopefully I can then do something to prevent similar disasters in the future, but this disaster is undeniably real and therefore is truth. I have only two choices then: make something worthwhile from the lemons in my life, or live in resistance to the lemons. One puts me back in the driver's seat; the other takes away my power.

If I'm having a particular problem with accepting something, I find it helpful to say this affirmation: *"the way it is."* This can be fun because when I say if fast, my mind hears the words alternating between, *it is the way,* and, *it is the way it is.* I begin to see that the way it is, is the way! It is the way it is supposed to be. From there I'm again in power to create something different. Another affirmation that had helped thousands is: *All is good—All is God—All is love.* I say these between twenty-five and fifty times when I need to get out of my resistance to *what is.*

ACCEPTANCE = FORGIVENESS

I was delighted to finally learn that acceptance and forgiveness are the same thing, which is sure not what religions teach us! We are always taught the one doing the forgiving is doing so through an act of kindness or generosity. That is not true. Nor is forgiving a deed the same as tolerating or coping with it; *true forgiveness is simply this: if you could go back and change what happened, you would not.* When you are in acceptance of truth: it is the way it is—it is the way, then you are forgiving and in turn forgiven; set free of the darkness that was robbing your soul of joy.

I know how hard it is to forgive someone, including yourself, who has taken something from you that you treasured. But hanging on to the fantasy of how it might have been, instead of accepting how it is, changes nothing, and drags you deeper into the darkness of resistance which weakens you. True forgiveness is saying: "I accept what happened and would not change it if I could." Until I am willing to accept reality in that way, I am not forgiving and I am powerless to build a future containing anything but the agony of continued resistance.

A farmer caught a vagrant stealing his chickens. The tramp was dirty, stinking and cold. The farmer took him in, cooked the chicken he killed, and fed it to him. Then he gave him a place to sleep. The next day the vagrant chopped firewood and milked the cow and had another meal before he went on. The farmer was not destroyed by the crime against him; he was empowered by it; he had moved his consciousness to higher level. Once the chicken was dead, he accepted that as his new truth and dealt with reality from there. He would not have changed it if he could. He accepted the vagrant as he was and forgave him.

Forgiveness and acceptance; those two are the same.

Nature is in a constant act of healing and forgiving. Every calamity in nature, whether it is a tree falling into a pond, a wild sea ripping up the shore or a fire burning a forest, begins healing instantly. Only we humans keep picking wounds open, refusing to let go of our past and move on. When we align with Nature, constantly healing and forgiving, we are empowered by Nature and flowing with grace.

On my fifteenth birthday I accidentally shot and killed Gary, my fourteen-year old blood brother, cousin, and my life's dearest pal. Gary was the only person who really knew me, my only confidant. We were inseparable spirits. After the accident, my mom gave me to Gary's parents, to take his place on their farm and replace the son I had taken from them. I packed my few clothes in a cardboard box and left my Mom, my brothers and sisters.

It was to be a painful time. Neither my aunt nor uncle ever accepted Gary's death. They insisted his bedroom, into which I moved, was not to be altered in any way from the way it was the day he left it. For the two years of long and terror filled nights I did my repentance by living Gary's life, sleeping in his room where his pocket change lay on his dresser next to pictures of his friends and his clothes were folded in his drawers and hanging in his closet. My clothes remained in their cardboard box on the floor. Gary's gun and tennis racket hung above the bed where I could watch them in the night, the same bed where we had lain awake for years, giggling and reading by flashlight.

My aunt and uncle were civil and courteous to me but cool. There was no way for me to be forgiven. How can you be forgiven for killing someone? You can repay stolen money or fix a wrecked car, but you cannot bring back the dead. It took may years to figure out the answer to that question. Until Gary's death could be a reality his parents and friends accepted the wound stayed open. I was there to replace their son, but instead I was the tragedy they felt and rejected every day.

My uncle barely spoke to me except to direct me to some additional chore. Often my aunt would see a boy in the market or on the street and clutch her breast, saying in a trembling voice, "Oh, oh . . . for a minute I thought that was Gary." And then my guilt would wash through me and my whole being would hurt; which was her intention.

Their resistance to Gary's death was daily resentment to me, thinly concealed but always there, like the dripping of cold water on my heart, not enough to talk about, just enough to wear me down. No matter how hard I tried, nor how much I sacrificed nor how blatantly I tried to show my love for them, there was simply no way to break down the wall between us. I was their prisoner and they were mine.

Over the years there were never any outbursts or accusations about what I had done; it was never mentioned by them and I was not allowed to talk about it. This penance fit exactly with my Catholic upbringing. I had been taught that to suffer was divine and that, because no amount of suffering would bring Gary back, there would never be a limit to the amount of suffering to which I was sentenced. So, even though my ordeal might have been the most awful thing a boy could go through, it could never be painful enough to erase my guilt, never enough to pay for the awful sin I had committed against my blood brother and his parents. Together Gary's parents and I did our slow dance over the years, never talking about Gary's body which lay bleeding in the middle of the kitchen table. It was continual, unspeakable grief. My aunt and uncle never cried, never said a harsh word to me; they were grim and silent and I choked on their silence. My loss, the loss of my pal, my soul brother, was never considered. It was just a part of my ongoing penance. During years of long sleepless nights, I ached for Gary's laughter, his close and fearless love for me. It was a longing steeped in my shame.

I didn't need them to openly accuse nor to berate me; I took care of that myself; as a well-trained Catholic boy, I knew how to torture myself. I suffered as much as I was able, especially during those eternal nights in Gary's haunted bed, watching the shadowed gun and tennis racket on the wall above me. I now realize it was not only Gary that died when I pulled that trigger, we all three died with him. If only we had known about acceptance and forgiveness. If only we would have understood that *It is the way it is—It is the way,* that *All is God—all is God—all is Love,* then we might have healed and been brought to an altar of forgiveness and realized a deep love for each other.

After two endless years, at seventeen, I found an honorable way to escape; by dropping out of school and joining the Air Force. But it was not to be that easy; both grieving parents traveled with me in my mind, and stayed with me through an endless stream of lonely, sleepless nights. I lay awake in my barracks, imagining Gary's body rotting in its coffin underground, wondering what state of decay it was then in. I let myself dwell on this because it made me hurt and I believed I deserved to hurt. I was sure I had no right to be alive. By not accepting what had happened and forgiving myself, I took my prison with me wherever I went.

It would take more than thirty years of suffering and self-torture, including years of clinical depression, panic attacks and living inside the Triangle before I finally discovered how forgiveness works. No priest, minister, counselor, psychiatrist or therapist ever had an answer to my need. It was only when I was near death myself, that I was able to look back and realize that it was all perfect. I suddenly saw that every thing that happened including Gary's death was a part of a beautiful and perfect pattern of life from which I was supposed to learn and grew. I now know that, it is the way it is, and it is the way it is supposed to be. It is truth—what is. I began to heal when I could at last say: "I accept what happened, all of it. I would not change any of it if I could."

Does it still make me sad to think of Gary? Yes, sometimes it is very sad. But it is neither dark nor depressive; there is life, truth and even joy inside my sadness. I could not have known then, that Gary's death would only be one of many dark events waiting for me on life's road. Each of them has been difficult, each filled with pain and sorrow and sometimes anger. But because I accepted them, each tragedy has expanded me, built a strength and understanding and moved on, leaving no residual darkness. These experiences continue to one dimension of the constant unfolding and romancing of my soul.

One value of these lessons has been the gift of helping others. For many years I have counseled those suffering was also from taking life as soldiers, policemen, murderers and those responsible for fatal accidents. I can help now, because I know how to keep those events from destroying us. I know how to heal them before they pull us into hell. It begins with an acceptance that becomes forgiveness. And it takes time and love.

No one sees the reality we see. No one else hears the music we hear or sees the colors we see. That is because the reality we observe is really our own reflection, like looking in a mirror. If we see a sunset together, I will see from the perspective of my soul and you from yours. We may enjoy it together, but we are seeing it in different dimensions; when we accept each other's experiences, we enmesh our souls.

When we accept others, a truly magic thing happens: they accept us in return. They almost cannot help it. They relax and make a place for us in their minds.

We are forgiven our debts as we forgive our debtors.

Respect

Because ARAS is a progressive process, Acceptance must be in place before Respect can work. After that, respect is the natural next step. What is respect? The acknowledgment that this person is singular, that there never was and never will be another of him or her. There is within this person a genius that cannot be copied, ever. Within this eternal soul is a nobility and light that is struggling to be expressed. No matter how dismal a person may seem sometimes, there is a soul inside in the process of fulfilling its destiny. The heroism of every being as he or she strives to overcome fears and demons during their own dark nights of the soul will never be known by anyone but them. The genetic talents and traits, refined by five thousand generations of grandparents, and passed down to this one individual, make him or her true nobility. None of these values can come to the surface or be expressed until there is respect from others. Respecting others gives them permission to express their greatness in our presence. By respecting we pull hidden treasures out of each other into the open and enrich the world. If we miss the opportunity to see that greatness, we will have missed an opportunity to see God.

Miss Brent, a kindergarten teacher was a quiet and unassuming woman. Only when she was encouraged by the respect she felt from her students and their parents did she decide to reveal her true self. She brought her handmade quilts from home for all to see. People studied the breathtaking colors and designs in awe and realized that their humble teacher was indeed a master craftsperson. Miss Brent's risk paid off by gaining her the respect of others while at the same time allowing her to respect them in a new way.

As I travel the world as a speaker and author, so often I am surprised by the enormity of character I find hiding in individuals, waiting for someone's respect to bring it out. As a firefighter and emergency medical technician, I found the heroism of dying or injured people always amazing. Again and again I was made to see that within each of us is a depth of character that seems boundless. Nearly all those I worked with who were facing death showed a grace and courage that surprised even them.

I helped a young Chinese woman give birth to her first child, carried a cholera-stricken sailor down a rope ladder in a stormy sea, watched a policeman gently disperse a crowd who jeered and insulted him, watched a woman give up her life so her children could get an education, held a woman bleeding to death internally, comforted a man dying from a heart attack and held a man who died after being thrown down a flight of stairs. Each of them was heroic and yet none of them would have gotten a second glance in a crowd on the street. However, if we could have known how magnificently their honor would shine during their hours of grace, we might well have been kneeling before them in respect.

We give medals for courage, skill, dedication, caring, and self-sacrifice to outstanding individuals, values we recognize in others because they reside in us, too. Medal winners are not extraordinary people, but ordinary people doing extraordinary things. By giving medals we show respect after the act of greatness. By giving respect we acknowledge greatness before the act occurs. Each of us, in our singularity, represents an incarnation of Great Spirit. No one of us can be replicated or duplicated, not even by cloning. There never was and never will be another you or me. As incarnations of the One Creator, we deserve each other's respect.

At this point of ARAS, a subtle but important shift happens. The first two words; Acceptance and Respect are *attitudes*. Now we address the second two words; Affection and Support. They are words that demand *action*.

Affection

The prerequisite for affection between any two people is *trust*, which is why acceptance and respect come first. Feeling accepted and respected relaxes our defenses, makes us feel assured and trusting of the one who is being affectionate. Trust follows acceptance and respect as naturally as morning follows night.

Some aboriginal tribes may sentence a member to death and then carry out the sentence by shunning. By shunning a person, all members of the tribe stop affecting him, shut him out from the grace of their souls as if he doesn't exist. The poor outcast usually dies soon after. Similarly, when a baby is not held, not allowed to give and receive affection, it will usually die. Studies on terminal disease have proven that many suffering from chronic illnesses are really suffering from a lack of affection.

Affection is necessary for survival of any species. Both land and sea creatures groom one another and do so affectionately. As humans we must either receive and give affection or fall out of grace. When you snuggle a baby, what do you feel? What could that warm sweetness invading us be other than the baby's affection? When not able to receive and give affection, it either will die or be deformed emotionally; or it may well become psychopathic.

Men, look at how much courage it takes for many of us to be affectionate, especially with each other. It's strange that the only place we can show affection to each other is on the sports field, where we unashamedly pat each other on the butt and say, "Good job buddy, I'm proud of you." Would a guy in the office try that? Why not? You see how jaded we are? We're lost in a world of make-believe John Waynes, and it is starving our souls. Hiding our affection from each other is not manly; it is a form of cowardice, though we glorify it by pretending we are too tough to care. Most of the world's problems are caused by men who deal with each other like stiff-legged dogs growling over a bone. If we intend to live to reach a ripe old age and do so in joy, we'd better start learning to be affectionate, to everyone. The Triangle gives us an excellent path for opening our hearts and romancing our souls.

Dealing with women can also be problematic; if you show affection for your secretary, does it mean you're trying to sleep with her? If you touch her shoulder and say "You look great today, sweetheart!" Will she think you are hustling her? And are you? Even if your intentions are good ones, she may have been taught all men are after the same thing. You might well find yourself in a meeting with your supervisor hearing about political correctness.

It is not only men who are afraid to let others get close. Women sometimes push men away who just want to be friends, and shun women who they are afraid will come too close. Isn't it their unworthiness that causes them to say:

"Oh, don't compliment me; I should have done much better!"

"This dress? This old rag? I should have thrown it away years ago!"

"Well, if you really knew me you'd see the world's biggest dummy!"

To be affectionate is to share the grace flowing through us and give life to those around us. What a great gift to be able to heal others just by caring!

Support

Support is loyalty. It is being consistent in the acceptance, respect and affection we are giving others. When you are confident of my acceptance, respect and affection, you feel supported. When I pledge my support to you, I am saying:

1. I will always express my acceptance, respect, and affection to you and welcome your expression of them to me.
2. I will *listen* objectively and without judgment to whatever you need to share with me.
3. I will keep whatever you tell me in confidence.
4. I will care about your goals and try to assist you in reaching them.
5. I will forgive you when you fail to meet my expectations.
6. I will hold a mirror for you to see your magnificence.
7. I will stand by you, even when others do not.

ARAS—Acceptance, Respect, Affection, and Support—this is Nature's way of relating to us; it is the way the Universe relates to animals and plants and all its other parts. It is the normal way our pets relate to us which is why we can always trust them. It is the same healthy relationship we must surrender to with each other if we are to reach our visions. On the Discovery side of the Triangle, ARAS is the outline for building a Support Team. In Self-Love it shows us how to love and be loved so we may restore ourselves and nourish our souls. I have used ARAS at government and business negotiating tables to bring polarized groups together. When one side wins at the exclusion of the other, some day, somewhere down the line, the score will be evened out; you can count on it. But when adversaries really care for each other and look for ways of winning that include, not exclude, each other, then negotiations become fun and exciting and everyone can win.

Note to Parents and Teachers:

While children still depend upon us to make their choices and protect them, before they begin to develop an accountable independence, it is important to reverse the order of ARAS and treat them with SARA: Support, Affection, Respect and Acceptance. The form will turn around gradually and as they mature. Children raised by SARA are automatically treating others with ARAS before they are adults.

CHAPTER SEVEN

CREATING OUR OWN REALITIES

◇◇◇◇◇◇

"Until one is committed there is hesitancy, the chance to draw back, always ineffectiveness. Concerning all acts of initiative (and creation), there is one elementary truth, the ignorance of which kills countless ideas and splendid plans: that the moment one definitely commits oneself, then Providence moves too. All sorts of things occur to help one that would never otherwise have occurred. A whole stream of events issues from the decision, raising in one's favor all manner of unforeseen incidents and meetings and material assistance, which no man could have dreamt would have come his way."

—W. H. Murray

The above quote has guided me out of a pickle and into success more times than I can say. Usually when I find myself being overwhelmed by problems, with no solutions in sight, I remember the line: *"Until one is committed there is hesitancy, the chance to draw back, always ineffectiveness."* Then I realize I am still on the fence, not completely committed. A star college basketball player came to me a while back with the problem of finding himself less and less effective in his game, his studies and his relationships. After talking to him a few minutes I discovered that his love and caring for his mother was the most important thing in his life. During our session he saw that his vision was for his mom to be out of poverty, living well. It was an easy step for him to realize that by getting good grades and playing ball at the top of his game, he could make his vision come true.

The simple fact of life is that *we can do nothing alone*; every achievement is the result of a coordinated effort between us and the universe around us. Even the grandest of us must eventually admit that every one of our accomplishments was assisted by something that empowered us, clarified our paths and made resources available when they were needed. Some say that it was luck, or knowing the right people, or being in the right place at the right time. Others might call it providence, God, the Universal Consciousness, the Tao, the spirits of our ancestors, or Great Spirit. But whatever name we give it, it is the intelligent and creative source of Grace that responds to us when we are committed. It is the moving power that makes up everything from a rock to a new idea. The Grace to create something new in your life *is simply not available until you are committed.* Will you please take a minute and read Mr. Murray's thoughts above once more? Do so slowly and see how powerfully this knowledge can change your life.

We remember from an earlier chapter that commitment is made up of two elements; intention and will; intention is the precise and absolute purpose with which we focus on accomplishing a goal; will is the hot forge of creation that brings that goal into being. Will, in this case, is also called determination. Intention without will, (determination) is not commitment, in which case the powerful and mystical force of which Mr. Murray speaks cannot be drawn upon. But when an intention is clear, the will is determined, and they are coming from a place of joy, the power of the entire Universe comes together in creation. When we focus on our vision, it must be with this intention and will; this commitment. Otherwise it is not vision, but fantasy we are seeing.

We must *see* our visions, our goals and hold that vision. All kinds of things are bound to come up. We will have good excuses for quitting, but usually it is just ego looking for ways to distract us to send us inside the Triangle into Paralysis. In a world where so many of us are comfortable with our fine homes, nice cars, and good incomes, security has become a narcotic that robs us of our creative passion. It becomes easy to just do what is necessary to please the boss or the neighbors. Then we must become excited about something bigger than we are, something worthwhile that frightens, yet thrills us, and we must take a Risk and say "yes" to the challenge.

I spent the early years of my life working to help support my mother and siblings. I kept a job and sent the money home even while I was living in Gary's place with my aunt and uncle. My self-image, formed early, was one of only being worthwhile when I was sacrificing for others. I came to believe that the harder I worked and the less I was personally rewarded, the more valuable I was. I grew up with unrewarded sacrifice feeling as natural to me as freedom does to others. I still believe in making my life a service to others, but I have learned that if I do not reward myself, my gifts to others will often become weak and maybe even bitter.

Then, when I was twenty-five, Mama died suddenly. The kids were taken by an older sister and supported by social security. My responsibilities were suddenly over. I was free to do anything I liked. The freedom was scary, unfamiliar, and confusing. I had walked with a heavy pack on my back for so long, I felt naked without it. For a year I tried to adjust to freedom. Daily I swam and ran and worked odd jobs to support myself. But without my burden, I felt useless and empty. I needed to be needed. I decided I needed a challenge to get me back on track, something to rip me out of my security and make me produce, something bigger than me, something scary.

I decided then, that I would become a singer. Then, with my fame and money I would be able to help lots of poor people, start education programs, and give to orphanages. Okay, good plan; I was on my way; I had the talent and I was willing to be committed. I had read and understood W. H. Murray's words on commitment and knew what I had to do. I made a vow: *I would do whatever it took, no matter how hard, no matter how long; to become one of America's most successful singers.* There's an important clue in this vow, and I wonder if you can find it; one that will shed light on the rest of this story. Here it is—I vowed to *become*, not to *be*, one of America's most successful singers. As we will see, there is quite a difference.

I quit my job, moved from San Diego to San Francisco, took a room in a cheap hotel, and grabbed every piddling job I could find to pay the expensive fees of my famous singing coach. I practiced for hours every day. Weeks turned into months, months turned into years, and I never let up for second. I stayed committed to my vision of *becoming* a successful singer. Disappointments, heartbreaks, being manipulated by agents and cheated by club owners became as dependable as the ticking of a clock. My real victories were almost nonexistent.

As time went by my expenses grew; I needed more and more money to pay for the voice coach and for musical arrangements. I drove an ambulance, worked as an emergency medical technician, drove a city bus, and taught first aid, modeled, acted in TV commercials, and worked as an extra on movie sets. I moved aboard a boat in Sausalito, started a truck-driving school, taught high school, took classes in drama and dance, and still worked constantly on my singing career. I lived for nearly an entire year on peanut butter-and-jelly sandwiches and two broiled chickens. I lost weight and looked like hell, but I didn't give up. I was committed to *becoming* one of America's most successful singers. Question: When does becoming turn into being? A question I never thought to ask.

My singing did improve, but my confidence before an audience dissolved as I became more and more internally focused and more of a perfectionist. Instead of the songs, it was always my voice I was thinking about; perfect tone, perfect pitch. As I became more and more critical of my own singing, my confidence drained until eventually I could no longer keep meter, the magical timing in music. I could sense the annoyance of orchestras and bands when I strayed so I practiced more and sang in public less. Without knowing it, I was replicating the first twenty-five years of my life exactly: I had great aims and worked as hard as I could, but was subconsciously making sure I didn't win, didn't get rewarded. I was still the penitent kid from the wrong side of the tracks, worthy of working hard but not worth having the rewards. I didn't believe for a minute I was worthy of actually *being* a successful singer.

In about the seventh year, things began to change. Jobs started coming my way: good-paying TV commercials, offers of parts in movies and appearances on nationwide TV. A wealthy group of lawyers decided to invest in my career. Suddenly I felt myself being launched into what I had dreamed of for so long. By now you won't be shocked by what I did next: I quit. Having no personal identity that could wrap around the successful lifestyle that was being offered, I left San Francisco, and went to sea. I took a job as deckhand on a dive boat out of San Diego. After many years of struggle, and finally finding success, I quit. Can you see why? The people who were trying to make me famous and successful were violating my subconscious (and true) commitment which was to *become*, not to *be* a successful singer. Can you see the difference? Have you let this sabotage happen to you? My romantic ego-identity was that of the *struggling* young artist and that ego was not about to have its identity replaced by that of a *successful* young artist. This happens subconsciously of course, otherwise we would stop it. We don't know why we suddenly become disinterested in that which we have worked for so long. In my case, the sudden aspect of actually *being* all I had planned for was too foreign and too scary. I went back to an old ego-identity I was comfortable with: I went to sea.

A year later I hired a young lady as a cook on my boat. She really couldn't cook in the beginning, but she was a wonderful kid with a charming personality and a real asset to the crew, so I showed her the tricks of the galley and she mastered them. As I got to know here, we dived together and became friends. She told me of her dream of being a successful actress and I could see it was not an idle fantasy, but a real vision. I told her of my ill-fated career and talked about how one might design a career that worked instead of one filled with self-sabotage. I have always hoped that sharing my experiences were of some help to her because it would give them value. My teenage cook, as good as her word, did follow her vision with clarity, courage and constantly increasing confidence and has become one of the world's leading actresses. I learned from her too; comparing her career to mine, I see clearly how different the results are when one is being instead of becoming. So here is our lesson: If we truly want to make our life's visions come true, we must build a psychological bridge between becoming and being. We can audition forever to become what we want but will never *be it* until we own that identity. Without the intention and will to *be, do* or *have*, there is no commitment, there is only trying, which is the futile effort that supports not vision—but fantasy. We can paste our visions and affirmations on the mirror and in our journal and repeat them two hundred times a day and still go nowhere, unless we are willing to *be* the dream. Devotion, allegiance, dedication, diligence, obligation, even vows mean nothing until we are committed. If we become committed to the struggle rather than the result, as I did in my singing career, then the struggle is what we get. What I really wanted, based on my results, was hard work and disappointment; a situation with which my ego had always felt right at home.

Subconscious intentions are powerful enough to heal us when we are dying or to kill us when we are well. Operating below the level of our awareness, the subconscious guides our lives on an autopilot programmed by our beliefs. It is the home of our prejudices and our biases and the foundation of our identity. When going after my goal, I was saying one thing consciously while subconsciously intending another. Intention always wins. I didn't get what I said I wanted, but I got exactly what I intended.

The question I should have been asking myself all those years was this: "Based on the results I'm getting, what must be my subconscious intention?" I would soon have realized I was off track, being guided by ego instead of vision. I needed the Triangle but it was not created yet. It would have taken me out of my self-defeating pattern and helped me transform my life to the one I was dreaming of. A way of always knowing where our commitment is focused is by realizing where our attention is focused. If our goal is on the far shore of a shallow river, we can surely reach it, one stepping stone at a time; the stepping stones are our mission. But, if halfway across we find ourselves teetering on a precariously balanced stone and become afraid of falling in, then our intention may change from reaching our goal to not falling in the water. We need to stop looking down at the rock and refocus on the goal.

Can you see how powerful that is—intention being guided by attention? When we have trouble focusing our intention, we need only refocus our attention and our intention will follow. We raise our eyes to the goal on the far shore and maybe we must step off into the current. The turbulence knocks us off our feet, but our intention is clear and our will is powerful. Will gets us upright again and again and empowers us onward to our dreams.

The power of one's will is amazing. Human history is filled with stories about heroic feats accomplished by willpower: a woman lifting a car off her child, a man staying afloat for days in a stormy sea, a child surviving for weeks lost in the wilderness. When we *will* something, we have unleashed a mighty, universal, creative power toward its creation—grace. When our intention and will are focused on a vision, we are committed and our success is almost guaranteed. We have an unbeatable team. When we are committed, we do not get that sick, panicky, depressed, or helpless feeling. We may fall on our way across the river, but it will not matter because failure is not in falling down; failure is in not getting back up.

One evening while I was on a speaking tour I received a surprise phone call in my room. Maddie, a student and friend, was in a hospital across the country. She was going into surgery the next morning for a large malignant tumor in her brain.

Here is our conversation as nearly as I remember it:

"Maddie, dear, what's happening?"

"They found a big tumor in my brain and they are going to try to remove it tomorrow morning."

"Can they really remove it?"

"Yes, but the operation will leave me blind and partially paralyzed."

"How do you feel about that?"

"I hate the thought of being blind, but what can I do? This tumor will kill me if I don't let them remove it."

"What do you want?"

"I want the tumor to go away without losing my eyesight or being paralyzed."

"How strong is your willpower?"

"Bob, I am so tired right now, I can't think of willpower."

"What is your intention?"

"My intention? I . . . I don't know."

"Maddie, I can feel your exhaustion. But if you can get a clear vision and become committed to it, your willpower can take over and might just make a miracle. Can you do that?"

"I don't know."

"Are you willing to take a risk?"

"Yes, but I'm so exhausted!"

"Do you think that might be emotional instead of physical exhaustion?"

"It might be."

"Do you feel your spiritual source? Is that river running through you?"

"No, I guess not. I feel disconnected. I feel like I'm being discarded."

"What can I do to help you?"

"Please, just give me some guidance? Please. I trust you. Help me."

"OK, Maddie, to begin with, please ask the doctors and nurses to not give you sleeping medication tonight; insist on it. Remember, it's your body and you're responsible for it. Be cooperative, but don't let anyone take over your life."

"Well, I guess that's what I have been doing since my divorce. Now I just don't have any spirit left."

"What does this tumor do for you?"

"What do you mean by that?"

"I mean, does it serve you in some way?"

"I can't see how."

"Does it punish you?"

"Oh, yes, I guess it does that alright!"

"What are you being punished for?"

"Oh, I guess so many things I've messed up in my life. . . ."

"Do you want to live?"

"Well. . . . for the past months I didn't know, but now I do. I do want to live. That's why I had them track you down."

"OK then, let's work together. Remember, doctors can do their part, but they cannot heal you; only you can do that."

"Well, I'm ready."

"Good. Lie on your back if possible, with your hands beside you, relaxed, palms up."

"I'm feeling better already."

"Good, try to relax your whole body, totally. Then you have to open your entire being to receive the blessings of the Universe, of God, of all the angels and of all your more than five thousand grandparents and of all your friends who have left this life and are now watching you from the other side, and of all of us who love you. Can you do that?"

"I'm trying. It's not easy."

"See them and us there, Maddie, all around you now, smiling and loving you."

"I can feel my grandmother here."

"Okay, now, repeat these words over and over to yourself: *I am completely forgiven for everything. I am a perfect child of the universe, and I want to live a joyful life.*'"

I repeated this and had Maddie repeat it with me until I was sure she would not forget.

"How do those words feel?"

"Real good!"

"Okay then, any time tonight you feel you might not have the right to be whole and well, please repeat these words until you feel this joy in you again"

"Okay."

"Now, imagine yourself driving down a street, Maddie. Look in the rearview mirror and see your past laid out behind you. See only purity: flowers, hedges, and a neat, clean street. If you see any trash, or anything that seems wrong, turn it all into flowers."

"How?"

"Just forgive it."

"Forgive it?"

"Yes, make it perfect just as it is; surrender to it. It only looks like trash because you are resisting it. Forgiving means you would not change it even if you could."

"Why am I doing this?"

"Because acceptance opens up your soul to the Universe and resistance shuts it down. In order to do what you need to tonight, you must be one with the Universe, totally accepting of all—just as it is. Keep blessing your past until you can honestly say, 'I want it to be exactly like it is.'"

"I'm doing it already. And I do feel stronger."

"Good, Maddie, good. Now, when the street behind you is clean, when your past is all flowers, stay relaxed, in an open-body position, and continue to drive along the streets of your life. Only now, please pay attention to where you are, and where you want to go. Set a goal and head for it."

"OK, I got it."

"Now, see a garden of joy around you as you go. Accept warm, bright sun shining on you as you drive. Feel it soaking into your body, healing you and filling you with light. Know it is Great Spirit, God, love, pure grace and all your ancient parents and grandparents sending you their healing blessings."

I heard a sob. "Maddie, are you crying?"

"I was remembering my mother. I haven't thought of her for so long."

"Your mom's not dead, you know. She left her body but she's here and she still loves you. Talk to her, Maddie. Tell her you need her healing touch, her grace. She has it, she can send it, but you have to tell her it is your will to be whole and well."

"I feel her here."

There were tears in her voice as she thanked me and assured me she would do what I asked. Then she asked another question. "What do I do about this tumor?"

"That tumor, if there is one, is made of light. Let it become one of the lovely flowers that you accept completely; love it for its beauty, then let it go. Let it dissolve, you don't need it anymore. It was just another temporary manifestation of light. Concentrate, throughout the night on the river of love and Grace flowing from the smiling heart of the God, flowing through your body. Concentrate on how well you are."

"What about tomorrow?"

"Tomorrow hasn't been created yet, Maddie. There is no tomorrow, there is only now. The enormous power of your will is only available to you right now. You can only create in this moment. So you don't have to wait for tomorrow; see yourself healthy and happy now."

I learned the next afternoon that, when the doctors opened Maddie's skull, they found no tumor.

I am not advocating that we ignore the advice of our doctors or try to cure ourselves without their assistance. We really do need their experience and expertise and must listen to them. But our healing is our responsibility, not theirs and the power of that healing comes from taking charge of our lives and making peace with our worlds. Our lives are our own. When our attention is on the beauty of the world, it is a beautiful world we create. Through the power of commitment, a new life opens before us, one in which we are free to create whatever we want. The two pillars of commitment are *intention*, and a *determined will*, neither of which are available when we are in guilt, loneliness, shame, resentment, or any unfinished business that eats at us from our past. At any time, we can accept and forgive the people and events in our lives and turn them into flower gardens. Then, in joy, we can focus our intention and willpower on being well.

A lady came to as seminar in San Diego and said she was there because her doctor told her she had cancer and only six weeks to live. After the seminar I didn't see her again for almost eight years, when she again showed up in a seminar. I asked her why she was there and she laughed and said her doctor had again given her six weeks to live. The last I knew she was years later when she was running a professional support program for cancer patients and doing well. She was not healed by me or my seminar, but by the truth she saw about herself as pure soul; when she forgot that truth, she came back and reclaimed it and was made well again.

CHAPTER EIGHT
THE CHAKRA CONNECTION

◇◇◇◇◇◇◇

Perhaps you have heard about, or even know something about the Chakra System, those seven energy centers that lie along the front of the body. It will take but a few minutes to understand how this system works and how it can benefit your search for self-empowering truth. The human mind is not contained in the brain; it is not even contained in the head. Your mind is a network of intelligent energy that lives throughout and around the entire body. Every single cell from the tip of your big toe to the top of your head is alive with its own unique consciousness.

Three days ago, a guy in the parking lot said something nasty to Barbara, Joe's girlfriend. Saying nothing to the bully, Joe quietly got Barbara into his car and drove away. But his gut would not let it go, a place between his ribs and his naval was churning with pent-up fury, almost more than he could control; the urge to go back and beat the guy to a bloody pulp was overwhelming.

Two days ago, Joe's mother fell in the grocery store and had to be taken by ambulance to the hospital. Joe felt his heart breaking, felt like he had been struck in the center of his chest.

Yesterday, against fierce competition, Joe's brother won the inner-city track meet. Joe tried to tell him how proud he was, but the words got stuck in his throat.

Today, Joe awakened to birdsong and sunshine, went out onto the back porch, and looked into the garden. The serenity made him sigh. Then lost, he stared in blank silence into the golden light. He was shocked when his father, sitting behind him on the porch, asked what he was looking at. He said he felt "heady."

In each of these events, Joe was experiencing the energy from a different chakra, or mind-body connection, and each of them had a value to him: they added to his soul's accumulation of wisdom and opened him up to life on an even greater scale. I have said that as we go around the Triangle, our life expands and elevates; if Joe accepts and adequately expresses these experiences they will have exactly that effect on him—they will make him a bigger person. When any one of those events, such as the one with the bully in the parking lot, haunt him, it is because he has not integrated that experience, he is still unable to "come to grips" with it. He is seeing himself instead of the bully as the principal character in the event, thinking that he must be less a man for not fighting. When he grows enough to get himself out of the way, he will see that the guy was very troubled and expressed his problems by being troublesome. (Troublesome people are people in trouble.) Then he will understand that it was just another step in his karmic staircase that he can leave behind and move on up. He will not want it to be different, he will have integrated it. Until then, that chakra energy will not be quiet because it is a part of him that needs to be healed in this lifetime. In healing this matter, it will not be okay for him to take revenge, to brood about it or, "to just forget about it." It must be integrated and forgiven. Expressing his grief to members of his support team will help him eventually do that. So we see that understanding chakras is important because they tell us whether we are flowing with grace or are stuck in those areas.

We are not our minds nor are we our bodies. We are souls who are in constant creation of minds and bodies so that we may experience and express and thereby grow. You, as soul, are projecting yourself out as mind and then you, as mind, create your body. This creation didn't just happen at the time of your conception or birth; it is ongoing; at every moment soul is creating a new mind and the mind is creating a new body. Since, on its fundamental level all reality is made of vibrating, intelligent energy, mind and body are indeed just different aspects of soul. As we go forward through this chapter, please practice actually putting your awareness on each chakra area of your own body. It will help you integrate the information you are reading.

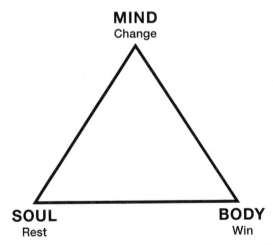

The mind is the creation of the soul. The body is the creation of the mind.

Joe was at first mentally, then emotionally, then physically stimulated by the guy in the parking lot and then wanted to beat the tar out of him. That would not have been an expression of his soul, but a reaction of his ego. He was dangerously close to getting out of control. Imagine a painter, filled with anger, furiously, yet creatively, channeling his anger into his work. Then imagine the same painter ripping his canvas to shreds. One is the way soul expresses its healthy anger, through creation; the other is the way ego expresses its anger, through reaction. When we understand how our chakras work, we can better understand how to channel emotions creatively, from the soul.

Chakras

Until recently most of us thought the mind resided in the head because that is where the brain is, but since the brain's neural network is actually throughout the body, we realize the mind/brain connection must be at various communication centers along the line of the body. These centers are called *chakras*. At each chakra point, mind and body are linked in a fusion of energy and information.

It is a commonly held opinion that we have seven chakras. Some of us believe there are more. These centers where mind and body come together are known by numbers.

- The first chakra is at the pubic level.
- The second chakra is halfway between the pubis and the navel.
- The third chakra is halfway between the navel and the heart.
- The fourth chakra, called the Heart Chakra, is at the heart level.
- The fifth chakra is midway in the throat at the Adam's apple.
- The sixth chakra, called the Third Eye, is at the center of the forehead.
- The seventh chakra, called the Crown Chakra, is at the top of the head.
- Here we will learn that there is an eighth chakra, called the Higher Mind.

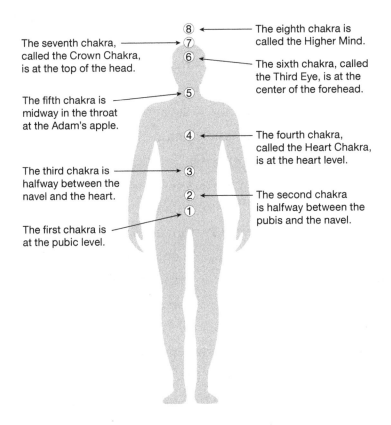

The seventh chakra, called the Crown Chakra, is at the top of the head.

The eighth chakra is called the Higher Mind.

The sixth chakra, called the Third Eye, is at the center of the forehead.

The fifth chakra is midway in the throat at the Adam's apple.

The fourth chakra, called the Heart Chakra, is at the heart level.

The third chakra is halfway between the navel and the heart.

The second chakra is halfway between the pubis and the navel.

The first chakra is at the pubic level.

Though the body seems solid, it is not. It is made up of a constant flux of energy and information. This combination is often referred to as Light, not that which comes from a light bulb, but pure grace. Your body is a cooperative collection of trillions of conscious cells, each of which is made up of molecules, and which, in turn, are made up of atoms. Each atom is made of subatomic particles, invisible units of infinite, intelligent energy. When we think of matter as solid, it is because of the limited way in which we see it. In reality matter is energy, held together in a universal plan. Our minds are in the middle, communicating soul's desires to the body and the body experiences to the soul.

Soul fulfills itself by receiving the results of body-mind experiences and expressions. It is always important to remember this point; we are here to experience and express and thereby grow in wisdom and joy. As soul you are like a plant that experiences the soil, sun and rain and expresses lovely flowers. Whereas a plant's natural expression may be flowers, a soul's expression may be the creation of art, music, literature or inventions, always reaching for ways to express the inexpressible and describe the indescribable. Like the plant, the soul is always reaching beyond itself; reaching for the Light. A saxophone player who hears a note in his mind so high and pure he cannot reach it, is stretching constantly to capture that note, but the dream moves away from his developing abilities like a rainbow before a chasing child. As our souls are always reaching for what is just beyond reach, the saxophone player's fantasy note is pulling him to a higher state of personal evolution. As souls we want to experience things beyond what we can even conceive, and in our quest we stretch beyond our comfort zones on a journey to self-realization. It is in this way that we evolved from reptiles to humans and to finally knowing that we are not primarily physical beings needing to feed our bodies, but spiritual beings needing to feed our souls.

The spinal cord ascends from the tailbone into the skull. Atop the spinal cord there is a knob. That knob was our first brain, our primitive or reptilian brain. The first and second chakras you see there were the beginnings of consciousness, connecting mind, body and brain together. As reptiles our consciousness was limited to eating, breeding, fighting and killing. We lived and died without ever caring about anything else. The ancestor with only these two chakras had no objective awareness of itself and no connection to others except through lust, hunger, rage and fear. Its body was wired to its mind through its two chakras and the command post was the reptilian brain sitting atop its brain stem. Even then however, this primary organ contained primitive rudiments of the limbic system that would someday become a feeling brain.

Over hundreds of thousands of years this ancestor of ours moved to the higher chakras like a carpenter climbing stairs as he builds them. At each level our awareness expanded and we were able to experience and express more fully. At each level, we needed to also expand our physical brain in order to anchor our awakening consciousness. The wisdom we gained at each level guided us to build the next step—always reaching up and so the body eventually changed from horizontal to upright. Energies and intelligence moved up the body from chakra to chakra in the way a tree grows, always reaching for the Light, as the brain continued to develop and coordinate new levels of consciousness.

Each chakra is the foundation of the one that is developing just above it. After, perhaps millions of years for chakra number one to create the one above it, the third was created by the grace of both of them, and took less time. The fourth, being created by the first three, was even faster. As intelligence and energy moved upward, awareness expanded and slowly became multidimensional, so that a creature might at first begin to think and, later begin to think about thinking and then to wonder about meaning. As chakras developed one on top of the other, so did new brains develop in teamwork with them, coordinating the evolving intelligence systems of mind and body.

Because a silent flow of creative, intelligent energy flowed upward from her base chakra, your great-great grandmother was always in balance, at first only physically, and then as higher chakras and brains gradually developed, was balanced consciously as well. We are still physically balanced by our second chakra, a fact you can test by standing on one foot and looking straight ahead. When you feel yourself beginning to wobble, touch your fingertips on the second chakra, halfway between navel and pubis. Focus there and you will find your body relaxing and coming into balance. From the first chakra, the flow of this energy, sometimes called chi (pronounced "kee") balances and heals as it rises through the body.

The business of the first and second chakras is survival. It makes sense, doesn't it? No future evolution was possible until survival was assured. In those two chakras and in the corresponding reptilian brain there is no gentleness, no love, no melodies or enjoyment of sunsets or rainbows. When creatures roamed the land with only these two chakras and their primitive brain-stems, life was a short-lived cycle of eating, fornicating, killing, and sleeping. If it was hungry it might eat its own young; it didn't care. There are many creatures on our planet today that have still not evolved beyond this level.

With each new chakra came an awakening consciousness that would, over millions of years, (evolution is in no hurry), create yet another and another chakra, a scaffold on which to stand while a new level was being built. The reptilian brain, like an outdated computer, could not keep up with the demands for higher intelligence so by the third chakra a new brain was developing into what would eventually become the limbic system. A new brain entirely, the limbic system did what its predecessor could not; it installed a new nerve network for the processing of emotions and thus opened the way for the best-known chakra of all, the fourth; the Heart Chakra.

Over centuries of slow development, the Heart Chakra sent its fires of passion into the darkness of the primitive mind, until emotions flowed like hot lava. New feelings were awakening: laughter, tears, grief, and loneliness. We no longer wanted to be alone; we wanted to share our lives and experiences with others. Emotions such as love, sadness, joy, worry and the thrill of sex were coordinated and fueled by the now active limbic system. This new, larger brain physically surrounded its smaller predecessor, the reptilian brain.

Each new brain and its coordinated chakras allowed the soul greater experiences and expressions. The mind was like a bird flying toward the sun, its very nature was to reach higher. The fifth chakra developed in the center of the throat, was the oral expression of emotions developed in the heart chakra. Those first expressions may have been grunts or moans but eventually became tone variations and primitive singing. With the limitless dimensions opened by the birth of music and intelligible communication, a vast new reality opened before us. This was the birth of art. The expansion of intelligence from subjective to objective, and from emotional to spiritual was beginning. The new chakra that would handle it would lie in the center of the forehead

Up to this point, the limbic brain had facilitated some communication, but what was now needed was a brain that could think, that could think about thinking, could combine facts to produce new understandings. This new brain, growing atop the limbic system, larger than both the reptilian and the limbic brains together, would be called the cerebral cortex.

The cerebral cortex was to the limbic brain as Einstein to Van Gogh. As souls we now had computers that could let us experience and express almost without limit, imagining things that never were and bringing them into being. We became creators, inventors, healers and knowers of things we could not understand. This expansion is also a problem because not everyone grows at the same speed. Those who lag behind are still sometimes relating to the world around them from primitive fight or flight mentalities. We have leaders who start wars because it is not in their understanding of how to accomplish their goals through higher means. But since we all inhabit the same society, the ignorance of one is often paid for by all of us, particularly when we are under the control of that misdirected leader. In our personal lives we are seldom becoming enlightened at the same rate as those we love, which is why it is important to always practice ARAS: Acceptance, Respect, Affection and Support. ARAS saves relationships that might otherwise be lost and makes it safe for our loved ones to grow at their own pace.

Now, let's take a quick review: The first chakra was survival; the second, balance; the third, the beginning of feelings; the fourth, the center of feelings; the fifth, the expression of feelings; and the sixth, the beginning of objective wisdom. We rose from survival to perception. Yet what we perceive in our newly developing brain is not always understandable. We are still reaching for the illusive musical note! Now a new brain, the neocortex, has begun forming above the cerebral cortex. Its coordinating chakra, directly atop the head, is called the Crown Chakra. When we focus our awareness in this place, emotions are quieted and we become observers; freed from judgment and allowed to see and know reality in a new way. The developing neocortex will doubtless take centuries to complete but in meditation we can already experience the purity of that consciousness as we move closer to pure soul-mind.

We have exhausted the body's chakras, the top of the head being the last physical outpost, but the mind can go where the body cannot; you can move to an even higher energy center, one that is purely soul, by putting your awareness at a place about three finger widths above the top of your head. We call this the eighth chakra or Higher Mind.

In Higher Mind, the time/space continuum becomes obvious, everywhere is here and all time is now. In this chakra, I experience bliss, a joy unlike any other I have ever experienced. As pure soul, I look at the world around me and at myself with deep appreciation and when I listen to music, particularly jazz, in my Higher Mind, I find myself in indescribable ecstasy.

So then, we see that the mind is not the brain, nor is it in the brain, nor a product of the brain. The brain, in fact, is a product of the mind, being created by mind just as mind is being created by the soul. The mind is intelligent energy, a field of awareness, moving through and around our entire body. The healthy way to live is to keep the grace flowing through all the chakras up into Higher Mind. But sometimes we get stuck on an experience and can't seem to forgive it. How many men are constantly in trouble for violence because they have not been able to move beyond their third chakras? How many people go from one tragedy to another, from heartbreak to heartbreak, their lives one long soap opera, because they never get higher than their heart chakras?

In order to evolve from a baby to a healthy adult we need to grow up through our chakras. To get from the base chakras to the Heart or caring chakras we need the opportunity to care and to be cared about; to exchange affection. In counseling of psychotic killers, it is a frightening experience to sit with someone who is watching you through reptilian eyes, completely unaware of what we call feelings. These are people who got stuck in their lower chakras at very young ages by being denied access to the Heart Chakra. Affection-sharing is necessary at any age of life but children must be allowed to develop it. When they do not get the Grace-boost to reach beyond the survival chakras, they may never develop the ability to love, to grieve or to care about another. They may eventually become predators; drug lords, gangsters, corrupt business leaders, politicians or even ministers. All share one thing in common; their paths to enlightenment have been detoured.

We do not abandon the heart, or any other chakra, as we move our awareness above the heart to the Third Eye, then the Crown Chakra and eventually the Higher Mind. We bring their gifts to the Higher Mind where the whole system comes into balance. Then we know and feel ourselves as pure, eternal souls.

CHAPTER NINE

THE HIGHER MIND

◇◇◇◇◇◇

A free diver is one who swims underwater holding his breath. I first became interested in meditation when I was a free diver, struggling to get my underwater time up to three minutes. For months I had been trying to figure out what was keeping me from holding my breath underwater for longer than two minutes. I realize now that I always felt a bit apprehensive as I tipped over to fly through the underwater sky. When soaring down over canyons or reefs, I was enchanted by what I was seeing, but I also felt uneasy. In this kind of diving, or in the open ocean, where the bottom may be hundreds or even thousands of feet down, I was always trying to beat the depth or the time of my last dive. I only partially enjoyed the freedom of my flights, because in the back of my mind was always the fearful ticking of the clock: How deep am I? How much deeper dare I go? How much longer till I must breathe? Is something dreadful about to happen?

Within a few weeks after I learned to meditate, within my apprehension was almost gone. I no longer cared how long I stayed down or how deep I was; I just flew and soared and felt free. I was amazed, then, to find that my underwater time was steadily increasing; not only that, but the sea creatures that used to flee or to hide from me, seemed no longer afraid. Large fish that used to disappear when I came down through their canyons would now swim toward me or follow just behind my fins, for dive after dive. Even whales and dolphins became friendly and let me swim with them. I was finally flying . . . finally at home in the sea.

This was all the proof I needed that meditation was good for me. Over the years since then, I learned various disciplines including what medical doctors call the relaxation response. I discovered that meditation is not the realm of one guru or another; but the natural state of any healthy mind. It is having one's awareness directed from soul instead of ego.

Over the years I moved to more and more demanding meditations, always reaching for that magic something that would take me to the next step, steadily reaching new plateaus of consciousness and creative abilities I didn't know existed. Then one afternoon, while meditating on my Crown Chakra, watching light flow in and out as I breathed, I felt myself drifting out of the Crown Chakra to a place above my head. I had discovered my Higher Mind, the eighth chakra.

Higher mind is pure soul consciousness. It is a place of meditation where, unlike other meditations, one welcomes all thoughts and feelings. In most meditations there is a constant struggle to end "mind chatter" and to eliminate thoughts whereas in Higher Mind all thoughts and feelings are invited. It is by the very act of being accepted into Higher Mind that a thought dissolves by itself. Higher Mind is a place ego cannot go, a place where we see reality without the filters of personal beliefs.

It is to Higher Mind that we bring emotion-charged problems and watch them become transparent and simplified as we move outside the Triangle and back onto our paths. It is here in Higher Mind that our addictions lose their holds on us and are replaced with the joy and satisfaction of being alive. Pictures of saints from nearly every religion have halos over their heads. Could it be that the ancients knew about Higher Mind?

As we recognize the true value and proper perspective of things from Higher Mind, stress automatically evaporates. There is no prolonged mental discussion of what's to be done about a situation, merely an, "Oh, now I see how it is. I'm grateful to know that."

Of the meditations I have practiced, I am most fascinated by what happens meditatively in Higher Mind. I like this meditation because I can get into the deepest place very quickly and can even be there with my eyes open, while lecturing or writing or doing other duties. When I am in Higher Mind it is as though lights turn on and windows open and I am in a place of extreme clarity. I become sharply aware of all that is going on around me and experience my environment as multidimensional.

Since, in Higher Mind there is no emotional stress, it can be difficult to get from a state of stress or agitation into Higher Mind. If our ego is attached to a situation that is bringing about stress, it will not be possible to go into Higher Mind. But if we can release that attachment, even for a few seconds, we can fly through that maze and land in bliss. In the early days of my Higher Mind meditations, I had to constantly remind myself that my anguish was not me; it was just an experience I was choosing.

Being in Higher Mind is not leaving one's body, not being on the ceiling or across the room as we hear of in near-death experiences. Rather, when I am in my Higher Mind, my body becomes like vapor and my mind is no longer restricted by physical limits. Worries dissolve. I feel completely enshrouded with peace and security and completely abstracted from the dramas of life. The stories, roles, and scripts that have dictated my state of mind are now separate from me. I can go to Higher Mind whenever I chose and stay as long as I like and bring the other seven chakras up with me. Being in Higher Mind not only makes me more efficient in everyday life, I am more peaceful and joyful and I see options and opportunities where before I only saw problems.

If it takes you a few weeks of practice to develop your pathway to Higher Mind, don't be discouraged; the goal is worth the task. Once you have paved that path in your consciousness, you will be able to go there whenever you want, with ease, and stay there as long as you like. It is the best way I know to be one with soul and in constantly expanding joy.

At first I was sure I got there only because of all the years I had been conscientiously meditating, and that only advanced meditators would be able to reach Higher Mind. But after two years of working alone with my Higher Mind, I took a chance. I was conducting a three-day workshop on Relationships in a lodge on the Oregon coast where the participants were aged 16 to 60, were not meditators and were not experienced with consciousness-expanding processes. If these students could get into their Higher Minds, it would show me that it was a discipline that could be easily taught and learned. But how could I validate whether they had really made it, or whether they had just gotten to another very nice vibration? I found my answer in realizing that in Higher Mind, problems, worries, and anxieties lose their meaning. When a problem comes up into Higher Mind, the most common reaction is: *It just doesn't matter.* I now feel free from my emotional attachment, and see that this problem is neither difficult nor perilous.

Okay, I would use that reaction as my test. I asked the students to think of their most prevalent worry, to share it with someone near them, and to rate it from one to ten, ten being the most stressful. They completed that work, and through a very simple process I guided them to what I hoped would be their Higher Minds. I let them bask in the peace of it for a few minutes, then asked them to remember the worry they had shared. I asked them not to go down to the worry, not go down to the place where it was embedded in the body, but to bring that situation up into their Higher Minds and there to look at it and then rate it again.

I was quiet for a few more minutes, and then asked that they open their eyes, and yet stay in their Higher Minds. We can do that, because unlike standard meditations, we are not focusing on a place, but actually *going* to that place: the eighth chakra. Having one's eyes open has little effect on being in Higher Mind.

The participants slowly opened their eyes. Then I asked the big question: "How about that worry you had? I went around the room and asked each person to share how the rating changed. To my delight, almost everyone in the room used the exact words I had mouthed to myself so many times: "It just doesn't matter."

I learned that the Higher Mind Meditation neither requires participants to be advanced students or even to know meditation. Nearly everyone is able to do it the first time they try. The problem has been convincing them to do it regularly. When he first went into his Higher Mind, a well known professor and scientist in the area of brain research said he was convinced that Higher Mind is the same pure alpha-wave state Buddhist meditators reach after years of practice. Unlike my students, however, those monks have dedicated their lives to being in that very special place. They have given up the ego attachments that compete with such peace and they remain in that state as much as possible each day. But a student who gets to that place without realizing its true values are: longevity, health, peace of mind and effectiveness in daily matters, may be like a visiting tourist who seldom, if ever, returns.

In Higher Mind, we see ourselves as stage characters, all in our places, each moving through our poses. From Higher Mind we realize we are not our roles, but that our roles and scripts are merely ways we experience and express and thereby grow. We see clearly that, if we are willing to let go of our identities, we can play any role we chose.

How to Go into Higher Mind

It is difficult to get into Higher Mind when feeling stressed, angry or otherwise preoccupied with negative emotions because we become attached to lower chakras and find it hard to leave them behind. We cannot force ourselves to be in a place of supreme peace, we must want it more than we want our dramas. Therefore, in the early weeks of building a path to Higher Mind, it is wisest to work at it when not stressed or worried. Here is how to eliminate stress as you make the journey:

Please sit in a comfortable position or chair, but not so comfortable you will fall asleep. Close your eyes and, by breathing slowly, relax your body, beginning with your toes and moving, breath by breath, up your legs until you come to the base of your spine and pubic area—your first chakra. Breathe softly in and out of that area relaxing it, and then move up to chakra number two which is between your pubic area and your naval. Again breath through that chakra until it is relaxed, and then continue to number three which is between your naval and your heart. As you breathe your way up the chakra ladder, make sure there is no tension or discomfort in any one before you leave it. If you should find an area tense, simply breathe through it until you feel the tension lift. Continue this process through number four, the heart chakra, number five in the throat, number six, the third eye and number seven the crown chakra in the top of your head. This process should take about five minutes.

Take three more deep, slow breaths. As you release the first one, focus your awareness on a spot just *inside* the top of your skull. As you exhale the second breath, focus on a spot on the *outside* of the top of your skull. As you exhale the third breath, move your focus to a place about three finger widths above the top of your head. This is your eighth chakra, your Higher Mind. You may find it helpful to reach up with your hand and locate that spot. Maintain your focus in that spot. Don't be concerned if you slip; merely return your awareness to that spot and keep it there. If you feel any discomfort or have an intruding feeling or thought, do not evade it, but rather keep it alive and bring it up into that spot, into your Higher Mind. After five to ten minutes, open your eyes but remain in your Higher Mind. Do not let the world you see pull you down; rather pull it all up, into your Higher Mind.

Later, after you have become comfortable with this process, try the following; See your Higher Mind as an umbrella of pure light that you will pull down around you until you are inside it as in a cocoon. Then you can say aloud, "I am in my Higher Mind." At a later date, you can pull it down around your entire world, your Universe. Remember, that umbrella can be as large as you like; the Higher Mind is limitless in both time and space.

Unlike other meditations, where it is important to clear the mind of all thoughts, in Higher Mind we invite thoughts, feelings, and ideas to come up to where we are. Usually they evaporate in the process, but always we try, so there will be no imposed limitations on the expansion of Higher Mind awareness.

A fun practice that will fill your body with healthy endorphins is to turn on some good jazz or classical music, whichever you prefer.

Close your eyes, go into your Higher Mind, and pretend that the music you hear is coming not into your ears, but into your Higher Mind, and flowing from there down into your body. This is an experience worth working for; one of the highest, happiest feelings in life. You will feel laughing, joyful tingling all through your body. You will actually be subjectively experiencing the passions of both the composer and the musician.

Higher Mind has no memory, so there is no comparative analysis of experiences. Every moment is the first and only moment of your life. Every experience is the first time, whether it's eating chocolate, making love, or seeing a sunset, if you do it while in your Higher Mind; it is the first and only time. Because of that, the aging process, hastened by the stress of memories, judgments and beliefs may be slowed or even reversed. In Higher Mind we see life anew and, in the process, become renewed.

CHAPTER TEN

YOU ARE THE RIVER

◇◇◇◇◇◇

O n a warm and windy afternoon years ago, I took my, then six-year-old, daughter, Chauncey Anne, by the hand and we went down from the dirt road together, through fields of golden, blowing light, riding like boats over waving meadow grass, to catch a trout in the clear water wandering there.

At the stump of an ancient tree, we stopped to look for hawks. But for the silken wind and the blackbird who claimed he owned that meadow, all was still. I asked Chauncey where the river was. She pointed ahead to where we knew the trees were reaching their branches down over dark, crystal pools. When we got to the water, I again asked her where the river was. "Right there, silly!" she pointed to the water. I took my canteen cup, scooped it full, and showed it to her. "Is this the river?" She thought and shook her head. "No. That's just water, Daddy; the river isn't the water."

"Then what is the river?" I asked, watching her closely as she looked first at the flowing current, then up at the trees and sky, and then all around us, turning slowly.

"I guess," she said, shrugging, "I guess I don't know what the river is." She looked expectantly at me, but I said nothing. After a moment she slowly smiled. "You're tricking me, Daddy, 'cause all of it is the river, isn't it?"

I just watched her.

"Yeah," she said finally. "I think all of this is the river."

Chauncey is right of course; a river cannot be just its water or its riverbed or its fish or birds or insects, or even all of that together, because the real river is not physical. The river is only the being created by all those parts singing in harmony. And the Universe is not any of its parts nor all of its parts, but what happens when all the parts are in harmony. It is the physical manifestation of Great Spirit.

We moved out from under the canopy of trees and climbed a small hill, up into a cloud-streaked, cobalt sky, and from there looked back upon the meadow and at the water flowing steadily and surely toward that sea that was awaiting it. The singing of blackbirds stitched all the colors and tones and movement into the tapestry we called the river.

I sat on the grass on the hill and Chauncey flopped on my lap. From there we looked out at our paradise; everything we saw and heard was part of the great hymn, yet each part also contained the entire melody within itself.

If a six-year-old does not see that truth as a profound mystery, why do we? Is it that we have forgotten what is so obvious to an uncluttered mind? We know now that no one thing in this Universe can exist alone; that if even the tiniest speck of dust on the farthest planet ceases to exist in any form, the entire Universe will instantly evaporate. The river of life is all its pieces and it is each piece. If we reject any one part of our lives, we lose the whole; a concert becomes meaningless sound, a duck is just bones and feathers, a pie is only flour and cherries. But when we accept all of it, in its entirety, life is the timeless, spaceless paradise that lives in a child's daydreams, in an engineer's inventiveness, and in a poet's soul and in the purest of love. To live in such a world of beauty and to have the courage to love completely is to live in constant romance where all doors of possibility are thrown open and we are set free to create whatever our souls desire.

And how do you begin such a journey? You begin by daring to keep your attention focused on where you want to go instead of on your doubts, and then by following that soul-path wherever it leads you. You will create your reality by paying attention to what you imagine; wherever your attention is focused, you will see your creation. Do so with joy and love and you will have created a paradise.

If you find it is difficult, look for those parts of your life you have not forgiven and accept them totally, saying: "If I could go back and change that, I would not, because it was a perfect part of my developing life." Sure, it may still be painful, but the pain must also be an accepted part of the whole. Why is this so valuable? Because, unless we are a part of all and allowing all to be a part of us, we become isolated from truth and have no more purpose than a feather without a bird.

As life is a gift, being presented to us by our ten thousand grandparents, who each in his or her time, strived to expand the consciousness they would then pass to the next generation, we are the recipients of their good work. Let us expand it again in our lifetime. You are the river, changing and growing. When you stop your natural flow, you stagnate and go inside the Triangle. Your security then must be in accepting that your path will always be one of change, of transformation, of you constantly blessing and letting go of *what was* in order to become one with *what is*.

Through the Triangle and other useful tools in this book, you may now create any reality, reach any goal and attain any vision. You have learned that there are victims and there are creators and that the choice is yours. By practice, you may dissolve the habits of helplessness, self-sabotage and self-doubt and become a miracle worker. I promise it won't be easy, but I also promise it will be easier than life has been inside of the Triangle. This journey will lead you to new friends, souls who are also on their missions, who will understand and support your vision. You will attain your vision if you live now as though it is already true. By surrounding yourself with those who believe in themselves and in you, you will be in the company of those who have journeyed from cave dwellers to astronauts in a blink. And your most splendid journey will have just begun.

The first step in making your dreams come true is to show up. That special mate, that job, that opportunity you want will not seek you out, you must show up mentally, physically and emotionally. If you have a clear vision, are committed to it and maintain an attitude of gratitude, all you need do is show up. Oftentimes all those difficult things you thought you would have to do, are not required, the Universe sees you there on the brink and does the rest for you. Just show up!

If you will practice making the three vital Triangle decisions of Discovery, Risk and Self Love, in every part of your life, every day, until those good choices are automatic, you never again need find yourself in the Triangle's paralyzing center. With new confidence, clarity and courage, your mission and your character will strengthen each day until they are of deliberate intention and of constant miracles.

May you remember that your divine purpose for being here is to fulfill the quest of your eternal soul, which is guiding you into that divine mission even now, reminding you that you are loved, blessed, safe and free.

The afternoon faded into night and Tia Maria sat quietly, allowing us to think about our lives. Her voice came from the deepening shadows.

"If you would have everything you want, you must first want everything you have. . . . and then let it go."

Then it was quiet again while we digested this thought. Her last words came from the darkness, but they illuminated and changed my life; "We are here to experience joy; which is just inhaling the breath of God."

CPSIA information can be obtained
at www.ICGtesting.com
Printed in the USA
JSHW050032091121
20315JS00006B/34

9 781722 505097